How Was School Today?

...Fine

How Was School Today?

...Fine

A User-Friendly Discussion Guide for Parents and Their Elementary School-Aged Children

How Was School Today? Fine.
A user-friendly discussion guide for parents
and their elementary-aged children
By Shannon and Peyton White

Copyright © 2010 by Shannon White
Published by: Integrated Life Enterprises, Inc., Mount Kisco, NY
www.integratedlifeenterprises.com

ISBN: 978-0-9844204-0-7

Library of Congress Cataloging-in-Publication Data
20109000076

Cover and text design: www.charette.org
Printed in the United States

We dedicate this book to the parents in both our lives:

Shannon's Parents, Ellen and Bob.
and
Peyton's Father, John.

Table of Contents

Chapter 7: The Big Stuff

Introduction

Why We Wrote This Book

"How was school today, honey?"

Kiss, hug…

"Fine..."

My heart sinks every time I hear it. How many parents have been met with these words after anxiously awaiting the return of their children from school only to be met with this monotone response?

> *"Why is my elementary school-aged daughter not talking to me anymore? What is she withholding? Is this the beginning of the dreaded period where I, as a parent, seem to have horns growing out of my head and my pre-adolescent daughter sees me as someone who is embarrassing or weird? Has my little girl suddenly grown up in front of my eyes?"*

I was shocked beyond belief one afternoon when I picked up my daughter Peyton from a play date and the other mother told me about a conversation she had overheard between our daughters. At the school lunch table some children in her third-grade class had asked a boy sitting next to my daughter if he wanted to have sex with her. He replied, "Yes."

That's right – sex in the third grade! It was further complicated because Peyton had already told me he had wanted to be her boy-friend for some time. He had been sending her notes and calling our home at ungodly hours.

After I got over the initial shock and repeatedly said "Oh my God!" I became curious. Why hadn't she talked to me about the incident over the two month period since it had happened? I realized that I hadn't created an environment for conversations like this to occur. I am a television news reporter and a church minister. Every day, I interview people for news stories or listen to people tell me their deepest fears and dreams at the church. Yet I was missing a connection with the most important person in my life – my daughter!

The simple "How was school today" answered with a "fine" became so frustrating to me that we went to a therapist to see if we could get help with the deep feelings that must be lurking behind it. I was also curious, and I admit somewhat jealous, to overhear her chatting on the telephone with her father about things she had not told me.

What was I doing wrong? Why was I working so hard with so little results?

"You're not asking me the right questions," she told me. "What questions should I be asking?" I asked.

This book began as a way to figure that out together. It has become a vehicle through which we have deepened our relationship. Our hope is that it will help you deepen yours, too.

I became a parent for the first time at forty. In my thirties, I was busy building my career and getting my personal life in order. When I had accomplished enough, my body told me it was too late to have a baby. Menopause had come early for me. Fortunately, I had always dreamed of adopting internationally. My dream came true in June 2000. I met my daughter Peyton in Moscow, Russia. She was just a year old.

By the time I adopted my daughter, I was ready to be a "conscious" parent. For me, being conscious means to be aware of what is happening in the present moment; not thinking of yesterday or tomorrow, but just what's happening right now. It also means that I am awake to the influences that my daughter is facing in her life and giving her every opportunity to talk about what works for her and what doesn't. Perhaps most importantly, being a conscious parent means being aware of what gets triggered in *me* when I am with her and how that influences our relationship. How does what she says and does or what she doesn't say and do, make me feel and respond? When she acts up, for example, do my own issues get triggered leaving me feeling attacked, judged, or powerless? If so, I am not able to give her enough space to respond with her own feelings, because it becomes all about me.

I can drive myself crazy trying to figure it all out or I can simply try another approach. I can allow her to tell me, in her own time, what is going on in her young but very complex mind. That's what this book is about: letting you in on what is working for us and not working for us.

My job as a mom is to watch out for my daughter's safety and well-being. One of the biggest challenges for me as a working mother is how to do that when I am not physically there all the time. But even if I had the luxury of staying at home, I still would not be able to protect her from everything, nor would I really want to. I want to raise her to make healthy and safe decisions for herself. If she never has any conflicts at school or at home, she'll never learn how to cope with real life, and I will never learn to let her go.

This is a book that my daughter and I are writing together to help parents and their elementary school-aged children, or "tweens," to begin conversations, continue conversations, or reintroduce conversations and take them to another level. This is not an "Everything You Need to Know About Talking with Your Children Guide." You know your children better than anyone, but this book is one more resource for busy parents who want to have another way to begin conversations with children who are encountering new things every day.

My daughter and I are writing this together because we think children might hear Peyton's perspective better than mine, and adults may hear mine better than hers. I like the adage, "Take what you like and leave the rest." We hope this helps all parents and children know, love and respect each other more every day.

In writing this book, we talked regularly about how to keep certain conversations, incidents and ideas private. My daughter was also concerned (and rightfully so) that we not embarrass anyone by using their real names in particular stories. The idea of the book is to develop trust so you and your child can form deeper, more intimate relationships.

Perhaps the biggest gift I received in this joint project is the deepening of our bond. It has moved our relationship to a totally different level. One night at dinner she turned to me and asked, in her coy way, "So, how was work today?" To which I replied, "Fine!" And then we had a good laugh together and talked.

Peyton's Point of View

This book will help mothers and daughters, sons and fathers, and all adults and the children they love talk more, if they don't already talk a lot. There may be something very important that makes a child sad or happy and if they don't tell their parents, then they wouldn't know about it and it could cause problems.

It's hard sometimes to talk. If you're embarrassed about something, or if you don't want to tell your parents because you think you might get in trouble if you do say something, or if you've kept something in for so long, you might want to keep it inside and not talk. The advantage of talking sooner rather than later is that maybe the problem can be solved and you can get congratulated if you do something good.

—Shannon and Peyton

Setting the Stage

As I have talked with other parents of school-aged children about what works for them to get their children talking, many tell me, "Children talk when they are ready." That may be true, but sometimes parents can tell if something is bothering their child. He or she may need you to help foster communication and open a dialogue.

One friend recalled when he was young he held things back from his mother. "She was a real yeller," he told me. "I didn't want to talk, and I wouldn't talk. A lot went unsaid during my elementary school years." "What would have made you want to talk with her?" I asked. "I don't know," he responded. "Maybe if I had known she wouldn't yell, but that never happened, and I didn't want to talk to her."

If you don't create a welcoming atmosphere your children will probably sense tension. When that happens you can talk until you're blue, but they may never share openly with you.

Another friend told a story about her teenage son wearing a pair of pants that were sagging and showing his boxer shorts. She went with her first instinct, saying, "Jim, you need a belt," which set up a mother-son interaction. He responded with an attitude of "You're not going to tell me what to do," as any good teenager trying to separate from adults would say. The power struggle continued. The opportunity to connect with her son was lost because mom wasn't able to get beyond the outward sign of what seemed unacceptable to her. Later she said sadly, "I missed out on an opportunity to see him, really see him." She felt that she wasn't able to value her son for who he was.

Certainly parents have standards. But what if she is right, and each moment only comes once and is a potential opportunity to either connect with – or miss – your child? When I think of all of the lost moments that I cannot recover because I was caught up in some silly external judgment of what I think my daughter should or shouldn't have been doing, wearing, saying or anything else, I am saddened. Hopefully, the process of writing of this book together will allow that to end.

A friend of mine told me about a recent trip she and her husband took to Nepal. Upon entering one village, little children ran up to them, gleefully crying, "Namaste," translated roughly as "The sacred in me acknowledges the sacred in you." Obviously these children, steeped in Buddhism, recognized their own sacredness, and because of that they were able to see sacredness in total strangers. They learned that message from the adults who practiced it themselves and reflected it back to their children. The result was a wondrous experience of hospitality toward my friends, who left there transformed.

When the Dalai Lama spoke recently, he remarked how much the West is preoccupied with the issue of self-esteem. He spoke about how Buddhists don't have a sense of poor self-esteem because they *know* they are a reflection of the sacred.

On a good day, when I am connected with my best or "higher self," I am able to be there for my daughter; to be loving, generous and kind. I am the kind of mother I really want to be. I know our interactions are life-giving and helping her to be a healthy, whole human being. However, when I am "off" – when I am crabby, hurt, angry, or my ego or pride has been bruised, I am useless. Unless I get back in touch with the belief that I am loved and that all is well in the universe, I am most likely going to respond out of my "lower self" which will leave its negative imprint on her.

The key is to keep learning about myself. What is it in *me* that keeps me from being as happy, fulfilled, and content as I can be? Everyone has "stuff" they're working out from their ancient pasts. I have been on a journey to heal the wounds of my own childhood for many years, determined not to pass on certain traits. But lo and behold, sometimes I find myself doing or saying something I heard as a child, and I know I have more work to do.

In the end, a good sense of humor is a necessity as a parent. Otherwise we may develop premature baldness from pulling our hair out! Being comfortable with your humanity is another. A wise friend of mine once said, "In the end, the best we can hope to be is a flawed human being." With all the striving to be perfect in our society, maybe that is one of the most important lessons we can teach our children. Here's to being flawed! Much fun on the journey…

How To Use This Book

As a working mother I often feel guilty that I don't have time to do all the creative projects with my daughter that I think I "should" be doing, and want to do. The reality is I just don't have the energy to do much after I get home from work except fix dinner and oversee homework. Believe me, that is plenty! This is *not* another activity book to tell you what to do with your children, although there are lots of ideas that have worked for us.

Each chapter contains several related topics and at the end of most chapters are the following thought-provoking features: *Try This*, an exercise for practical application; *Peyton's Point of View*, where Peyton offers her unedited thoughts to other children on a particular discussion topic; *Questions for Reflection*; and *Did You Know*, related fun or interesting facts.

This book is designed to be used in small doses, perhaps during dinner, at bedtime, in the car, or any time when you have a few uninterrupted minutes to talk. The Questions for Reflection at the end of the chapters provide opportunities to ponder the material either then or at another time. Sometimes questions are for parents only, while others are for parents and children together. Peyton and I have some of our most profound conversations on Sunday mornings while driving to church. Since I am looking straight ahead and she is sitting in the back seat, she has a sense of anonymity and some space to share more personal things.

For centuries, authors of religious and popular literature have used the tool of story to let a reader "overhear" a situation and affect change in their own lives. We have included stories from various traditions and provided some reflective questions to use, again, as conversation starters.

You won't relate or agree with the approach of every story or situation. That's okay. Every family is different, but we can all relate to similar feelings. We encourage you to identify with the feelings of what you read, versus comparing your story and discounting it because it is not your experience. You may say, "I'm already doing all that." We say, "Great!" Keep up the good work and let us know what works best for you.

Let the conversations continue!

1

Home and Family

Creating a Family Climate

The twenty-first century family comes in all shapes and sizes. Long gone are the days of the nuclear family norm consisting of father, mother, and two kids all of the same faith and cultural background. Today some families have children in different developmental stages; step-parents and step-children or his/hers/ours; grand-parents raising grandchildren; foster parents and foster kids; two dads or two moms in one household; multi-racial backgrounds or multi-faith backgrounds; single parent heads of households; both parents working outside the home and a live-in nanny; extended family live-ins; adopted and/or biological children; children born with the help of modern science. And more! No one can make generalizations about what constitutes family, and that may be good because it requires us not to make assumptions when we speak of "family."

I am a working, single mom with only one daughter to raise. When I was married, our family included six children spanning thirty-three years in age. Some were married or had significant others living nearby who we saw regularly. Former spouses were included in holiday and special events. Life was full.

My life during and after marriage are two very different models of family. Both are legitimate. Each family determines for itself the climate of what works and what doesn't in order for each member to feel a sense of connectedness and belonging.

Managing a household while raising healthy children is a monumental task. I am in awe of those who have multiple children near the same ages. Here's one example of a real supermom: Susanna Wesley lived in the seventeenth century and bore nineteen children, ten of whom lived to adulthood. Since her husband was a busy preacher, and had the reputation of being somewhat difficult, most of the child rearing and household management fell to Susanna. The family had many challenges such as deaths and fire, as others did in those days. Yet through it all, Susanna spent regular, individual time with each of her children. When I think of what it must have taken to keep track of ten children and give them what they needed, I have no room to think about being tired at the end of the day! Susanna's persistent dedication paid off as her children grew into adults. Her sons John and Charles became two of the great leaders of the Methodist church.

Most families in this day and age don't have that many children, with the exception of reality TV stars! But even for small families, communication is essential in managing multiple schedules and meeting the needs of each member of the family.

Family Meetings

Many parents use regular family meetings to keep the channels of communication open. The idea is to have a regular time and format so that members of the family know what to expect; if something comes up during the week, they know they will have the opportunity to bring it up at the meeting. Weekly schedules, family decisions both big and small, expectations, and any other communication which needs to take place can all be discussed. Families can set up their own guidelines as to what types of issues and topics will be discussed as well as how the meetings will be run. For example, does everyone get an equal "vote" if a decision needs to be made, or do the parents have the ultimate say? How will you ensure that everyone feels heard? Older children and teens may balk at the idea of having a family meeting if they are not used to it. But if they are run fairly, family meetings can teach negotiation and group processing skills.

As children get into elementary school, activities around meals can be community-builders. One mom with three girls in elementary school assigned her children to make dinner together on the nights she taught piano. Another mom with triplets assigned each of them a night to cook and a night to clean up afterwards. Now as teens, they look back with gratitude not only for having learned to cook at a young age, but for the nightly bonding time.

How and when do you connect as a family? What's the mood like at your dinner table? Is the television on, or is there time for each person to talk about what happened during the day? Many families are not able to have a consistent time to sit down, and some aren't able to sit down at all on a regular basis because of after school sports or other activities. But finding what works for your clan is important.

Peyton's Point of View:
Family is important because everyone sticks together and no one gets left behind. You have people who love the real you and not people who just think they know you. They will always be by your side even if you do something bad or wrong. They know you the

best. Sometimes your family includes people who care for you and who are nice to you.

Questions for Reflection:
1. What does family mean to you?
2. What does it take to keep your family unit together and connected?
3. What activities or situations keep you from feeling connected?
4. What needs to happen for you to keep connected when schedules get hectic?
5. What kinds of activities bring you closer together and when do they happen? (For example, playing board games, shooting hoops, vacations.)

Siblings

Families with more than one child provide instant community and opportunities for learning and bonding. In former generations, people had multiple children because they needed help with the family farm or business.

I love being a part of a large family. I am the second of four daughters, but there is a gap in our ages of eight and eleven years between me and my two younger sisters. When we were young, my older sister and I were often responsible for babysitting our younger sisters. That had advantages and disadvantages. We had a huge crowd of potential babysitting clients because of our sisters' friends, but we also had to contend with questions to visiting boyfriends such as, "Are you going to marry my sister?" As we have become adults, we have grown closer and the age difference has faded. I value and respect each of them for the women they have become. No matter how far apart we may be geographically, we know we are there for each other.

Families with multiple siblings have a whole feast of issues and challenges which can be great fun as well as frustrating. They provide the first opportunity for children to learn about living in community with other people. Human beings are meant to live together. Family life gives us opportunities to learn communication and negotiating skills, self individuation (how I am alike and different from you), generosity, and love. There can be times of harmony and there can be times of discord. How a family deals with each of these situations is what matters. Parents can set the tone and provide boundaries so that everyone's needs are met.

Keeping it Age-Appropriate

If there is an age spread between children in your family, it can be challenging to keep conversations, music, television programming, and movies at levels which are suitable for the different ages in your house.

It's perfectly normal for high school and middle school-aged kids to have friends over for parties, but that doesn't mean your younger children should be around to see what's happening. Do you remember what *you* did at those parties?

My mother used to warn me and my older sister when we verged on inappropriate territory around my younger sisters. "Little people have big ears," was her code phrase that meant *stop*! While it may be inconvenient to redirect a conversation in the presence of younger siblings, you are protecting their innocence and allowing them the same freedoms your older children had when they were young. Children grow up far too fast and will be exposed to many different ideas in time. You don't need to hurry the process and cheat them out of their childhood.

Sharing

The only way we learn to share is by doing it. When you're in a family with multiple children this starts early. Toys, clothes, and a parent's time are all things which have to be negotiated. As children grow up the challenges of what belongs to one child verses another may be harder. For instance, if rooms are shared, how does a child keep his own things separate? Parents can be helpful in setting the tone for this and making sure the boundaries of each child are maintained. For example, if Susie has a favorite toy, Jenny doesn't get to play with it unless Susie says she can. However, if Susie never lets Jenny play with anything of hers, that's another issue.

Fighting and Competition

One issue among siblings is the competition which can exist between them. Some children grow up feeling inferior to another sibling due to different abilities in school, sports, or personality traits. Jack may feel he's not as smart as Jerry who gets straight A's in school. But Jack may excel in sports. Those feelings may be reinforced by a perception that Mom or Dad loves another child more. We've all seen it and heard it. Conversations such as, "I always knew you were Dad's favorite," can continue well into adulthood. Some parents connect more emotionally with one child than another, due to similar personality types. Parents have to be extremely careful to love equally.

Remember the Biblical story of Jacob and Esau, who were fraternal twins? Jacob was closer to his mother Rebekah, and Esau to his father Isaac. Esau was the older of the two and was in line to receive his father's birthright, which was the custom in that culture. When Rebekah heard that Jacob would not receive the birthright, she helped him trick his brother out of his inheritance which was a coveted blessing upon his future offspring. When Isaac and Esau discovered the trick, they both were angry. Esau even threatened to kill his brother, so Rebekah helped Jacob escape. Jacob goes on to live the blessing he was given but with lots of struggle. It was decades later and well into their adulthood when the two reconciled.

One mother told me her twin boys are very different and very competitive. She handles the situation by explaining that even though they popped out within minutes of each other, each has different strengths. One day her son Dan remarked, "John doesn't read as well as I do." "Yeah," she said, "and he's working really hard to get better. He's really great at math, isn't he?" Mom acknowledged and celebrated the differences of each son's strength to the other. There was no pretending that they were supposed to be alike. What a concept!

When her boys fight, their mom said she has them stand together and hug until they say they're sorry. She says that usually within minutes they're giggling and apologizing! "This is it, guys...when Mom and Dad die, you'll only have each other...so Smiths stick together!"

As children get old enough to start hiding behavior from parents, they may begin to leverage what they know. "I won't tell Dad you did this, if you don't tell I did that." Parents need to keep an open ear to make sure this doesn't get out of hand. Watching interactions between children to make sure the power in their relationship is shared will give you a clue if something is off balance.

Did You Know?

There is actually a way to fight fairly with peers/siblings. Here are some ideas.
- Stick with "I feel" statements instead of blaming, such as "You did this..." It sounds like this: "When you did _____, I felt_____.
- Don't call the other person names.
- Don't grab or touch them in a mean way during your disagreement.
- Listen to what the other person is saying. When they are finished, take your turn.
- Take a break if you need to.
- Get an adult to help if you need to.

Ideas for Fostering Sibling Relationships
1. Take an "unplugged" vacation, such as camping, where there are no distractions, but only time together.
2. Have a family game night at home with no interruptions.
3. At the dinner table, take turns going around the table and have each person ask the person on their left about their day.
4. Make sure each child hears you complimenting the others as well as him.
5. Have regular family meetings to discuss the concerns of any child when they arise.

Peyton's Point of View

I like having siblings because they always help you out and play with you. My sister braids my hair, and my brothers pull my pony tail and give me wedgies ... yeah. I love them because they're comforting to me. I especially love getting together at holiday time. It's also hard sometimes with siblings. I have a hard time when they're talking to my dad and I need to tell him something. But I've learned to ask when they're finished if I can have his attention.

Questions for Reflection:
1. Do you feel love *for* your brothers and sisters?
2. Do you feel love *from* your brothers and sisters?
3. How do they let you know they love you? How do you show them?
4. Do you feel that Mom or Dad loves anyone more or less?
5. If yes, how do we communicate that to you and your brothers and sisters?
6. How do you see Mom or Dad valuing your own unique talents and gifts?
7. What's the best thing about your brothers and sisters? Name something about each one.
8. If you could change anything about the way our family works right now, what would it be?

9. Do you feel you and your brothers and sisters have equal access to me? Do I listen to one more than another?
10. When you fight with each other, do you fight fairly?
11. How do you resolve the fights I don't know about?
12. Is there anything that needs resolving right now?
13. Do you feel your property is respected by your siblings? Do you respect their things?
14. What does it mean to share in a family?
15. Is there anything else you need to say to me right now?

When We Struggle: Fighting Fairly

One of my favorite sayings is, "My parents push my buttons – and they know where they are because they installed them!" The struggles we experience with other people throughout our lives may be the outgrowths of what became "button-installations" when we were young. For example, if your mother was extremely critical and made you feel diminished as a child, you might grow up with issues around needing to be perfect. If your father was a workaholic and never around for you, you might have issues with abandonment. What buttons are you installing in your children right now? And is there a way to uninstall those buttons before they become permanently ingrained in your child's psyche?

Peyton and I started "power struggles" by the time she was a toddler. We're both strong-willed and knocked heads over what seemed to be silly issues. I foresaw it getting much worse in the future. I knew something had to change or the teen years were going to be a real headache. And I also knew that there was something about the way I interacted with her which set things off. My strong-willed spirit was rubbing up against hers. Somehow, her father had a knack of diverting the struggle. I was amazed as I watched them interact. I wanted to know more about how he interacted with her.

Somewhat desperate, and in an effort to change the dynamic, I signed up for a class called "Systematic Training for Effective Parenting" when Peyton was seven years old. The class, offered through a local drug and alcohol prevention program is designed for parents with children of different age groups. Classes are taught by trained leaders contracted through schools or other organizations. (For more information see www.STEPPublishers.com).

In the parent handbook they say in the course you will learn that:
- Your parenting challenge is to raise a confident, responsible child
- Your job is to guide, not to punish or do everything for your child
- You can expect your child to cooperate
- Your child's behavior always has a purpose
- Your family can work, grow and play together

The skills I learned in the course started to turn our struggles around within a few weeks, by changing *me* and the way I related to my daughter. I was taught to give my daughter more responsibility for her choices. When I started doing that and letting go of some of my controlling behavior, she stepped up to the plate and became more responsible. She also relaxed and trusted me more. It was somewhat miraculous. Instead of needing to be *right*, my focus was on giving my child the opportunities to learn from trying different choices and taking responsibility for the results, within a safe environment.

The experience reminded me of how a mobile works. When one piece of the mobile is moved, the rest of the mobile adjusts to bring it back to a stable state of equilibrium. As an added bonus, my new-found way of being carried over into my other relationships where I had been too invested in controlling a certain outcome. It was a win-win for everyone.

We still work at this. Different struggles affect us at different ages. As Peyton matures and new fears pop up within me, I have to readjust and rework my responses and ask for help. I continue to work very hard to release my tendency to hold on and control, which is one of the buttons "installed" in me early on in life. I check in with Peyton every once in a while to ask her how she thinks I'm doing. This also shows her that I can be a life-long learner.

Conversations with Peyton

Struggles between parents and children are normal, but they can be excruciating. Perhaps one of the hardest things to do is to disengage before you get the inner "tug" to struggle. Several months after I returned from a week-long seminar in which I dealt with some of my residual emotional issues, I asked Peyton how our struggles affected her. This was our conversation:

SW: What happens for you when we struggle?

PW: I feel sad and scared and like I'm in a little turtle shell.

SW: How can I find you there? What would make you

want to come out?

PW: Tone it down and don't yell so much.

There it was again – my yelling and frustration getting in the way. Ugh. At least she has the ability to describe it. I finally got to the point of telling her to let me know when my tone was getting out of hand. The permission to have her correct me has turned some of it around. Now if I start reacting over something, she'll say, "Tone, Mom, tone!"

As the pre-teen years continue, I wonder how it will progress…

SW: Do you think as children get older they have to fight

with their parents?

PW: They don't have to. It's really the children and how

they decide how to be good…how they decide

whether to do the right thing or get into trouble.

SW: Why do you think sometimes children choose to do the wrong thing with their parents?

PW: Because of peer pressure.

SW: How do you think I can support you as you get older?

PW: You can sort of help me by telling me the good things and privileges about being an adolescent. I don't know what else.

Questions for Reflection (for parents):
Here are some questions to consider that may help give you a "beat" before reacting to a situation with your child.

1. What is the emotional state of all involved right now?
2. Would a "cool down" period help in creating success?
3. What assumptions/interpretations are you making in this situation?
4. Is anyone "right" or "wrong" in this situation?
5. Is there another solution for this problem?
6. Would this encounter have the same intensity if a friend/ spouse/partner were dealing with this situation?
7. What difference would 24 hours make in this situation?
8. Can you raise/lower the level of discussion in this struggle in any way?
9. Is there any choice/power that you can give to your child to help them take more responsibility for their own outcome?

Adult Fighting in Front of Children

Children learn from what they see. There seem to be two schools of thought about the wisdom of fighting with a spouse in front of your children. One is to never let children see an argument between parents, and the other is to show children that parents can disagree and still love each other in the end. Certainly there are those who will take either of these options to an extreme. My thought is this: if children don't see parents modeling how to disagree without arguing and still remain in relationship, how will they learn to do it themselves? A clear distinction must first be made in front of the children between an argument and a disagreement. People will always have disagreements over ideas and opinions. That's human. Arguments take it to a different level and can be destructive. The key here is that any fighting must be fair.

So just what does it mean to fight fairly between adults?

- Stick to the issue at hand. Don't bring in the kitchen sink, i.e., "Last year, when you…"
- Listen without interrupting (even if you have to sit on your hands and bite your lip!).
- When it's your turn to speak, use "I feel" statements vs. blame – no "You made me…"
- Don't call the other person names.
- Don't use threats such as "I'm going to leave if you…"
- Don't attack the person, get to the behavior. The disagreement is mostly about what someone has done versus who they are as a person. Every person deserves respect.
- There's a great saying: "Say what you mean, but don't say it mean." Tone is everything.
- Be truthful and don't exaggerate.
- Humor helps diffuse a situation.
- Agree to disagree, if you need to. There is always more than one way to see some issue. There does not have to be a winner and a loser. Both are entitled to an opinion.
- Take a break from the disagreement if you need to, and agree when you will come back and finish.
- Keep it private. Not all topics are appropriate for children to overhear, no matter how civil it is.

"Take what you want and leave the rest" is a slogan from twelve-step groups. It simply means to evaluate what truth there is in what the other person is saying, and recognizing their "stuff" that you can let go. Just because someone says something about you doesn't mean it's the truth, but there might be some nugget which can help you grow.

Try This:
- If both parties are willing, sit close to each other and even have some physical contact during the disagreement. This communicates that you have the intention of working through the situation and getting back to closeness, without it leading to something sexual.
- Take a few moments in silence before beginning as a way to set the discussion on a spiritual plane.

Peyton's Point of View
It's not very fun for children to see their parents fighting. It makes us sad to see them fighting. It makes the children wonder, "Are my parents ever going to stop fighting?" I want to say to them, "Why are you fighting? And why do you want to fight in front of me because it makes me sad and scared."

If your parents are fighting, it will be okay. They'll get through it. Ask your parents to stop and tell them how it makes you feel.

Questions for Reflection:
1. How do you feel when Mom and Dad fight?
2. How do you feel when we disagree?
3. What does it communicate to you?
4. Do you ever worry that you are to blame for our fighting?
5. Do you know how we feel about each other?
6. Do you feel that our (parent and child) disagreements are fair and that you are heard? If no, what can I do so that you feel heard and understood?
7. Have you heard me apologize to you when I have been wrong?

8. What can you do to help the situation when we struggle?
   (Both answer)

Mom is Wrong...a Lot

Many of us grew up with parents who never admitted they were
wrong. It just wasn't done. My parents were young when they had
me and still young when I was old enough to challenge what they
were saying … and boy did I ever.

Times are different now, and it is more acceptable for parents to admit
when they have made a mistake in judgment or action. In doing so,
you give your child permission to see you as human. They see that
making a mistake is not the end of the world, and relationships can be
repaired if a heartfelt apology is given and actions are changed.
So I apologize to Peyton for yelling at her, instead of explaining
away my feelings. I give myself timeouts when they are appropriate, to show her I hold myself to the same standards of conduct as
I do her. She holds me accountable, too.

One day, Peyton and I went into a shop to buy a thank you
present for a friend. We picked out a fruit arrangement and I was
surprised at how much the clerk said it cost. It was more than
I wanted to spend, but we went up to the register anyway. I felt
ashamed that it was too much for my budget and mad that Peyton
wanted to get it for our friend. "Cash or credit card?" asked the
clerk. "Cash," I told the woman and proceeded to write a check. I
handed it to the woman, who said in an annoyed voice, "Oh, we
don't take checks." "I wish you had told me that before I wrote out
this check," I replied in my nicest, passive-aggressive voice. "I did
… I said 'cash or credit' and checks are not cash," she said, even
more annoyed. "In some places they are seen as cash," I snipped
back, as she walked away from the register. I said, "Thank you. I'll
think we'll go somewhere else" And we left the store. Not one of
my finest moments.

As we got into the car, I thought, *What just happened there?* I asked Peyton the same question, not expecting her to answer. Peyton said, "She was kind of rude." But I knew there was more to it and I was the one at fault here, regardless of what the store clerk had said. "I didn't do too well with that interaction. How do you think I could have handled that better?" I asked. Immediately, without looking up from her Nintendo DS, Peyton said, "You could have said, 'Oh, I didn't know you couldn't write a check.'" Wow. "You're right," I said, "That would have handled it. Mom was wrong. Thanks for your suggestion."

I had a choice. I could have bad-mouthed the clerk afterwards and made her look wrong by giving my "spin" on the situation, or talk about it as quickly as possible and take responsibility, which I did. Even though my pride was hurt by not being able to afford the gift my daughter picked out, the more important thing was I had been able to step outside my inside "stuff" and reflect on what was actually going on. Most important of all was that I was able to admit I was not doing it well, and give Peyton an opportunity to help me problem solve.

Later, we did try to go back so that I could apologize, but the woman had already gone home. I never went back in, but when we passed the store months later, Peyton lovingly reminded me, "Remember when we went in that store and you and the lady got into it? You were going to apologize." Right again.

Why is it so hard for most people to accept their frailties to themselves and others? In my case for many years I was too fragile inside to admit it. Blaming others and trying to make myself look good was the only way I was able to make sense of certain situations. When I finally let go of my need to be perfect, that the world would not end if I admitted my responsibility, things became easier. My relationships became easier. I became part of the human race.

Then I realized, it doesn't cost me anything to say I'm sorry to someone. Sure, maybe my pride, but that's a small price to pay for the healing that can come to a damaged relationship. But if you say you're sorry, you have to mean it, and you have to stop what you're doing that caused the pain to the other person.

Did You Know?
In both the Hebrew and Christian traditions, repentance is key to the act of forgiveness. It actually means a "turning" of behavior. So in order for forgiveness to occur, the behavior which caused the break in the relationship must first stop and change. Then the hurt person can complete the act of forgiveness.

Peyton's Point of View
It's very important to see that mom makes mistakes and admits them, because it makes me feel that everybody makes mistakes in life, not just little kids. All kids think when they make mistakes is, "Am I going to get in trouble?" and they don't want to admit it. But all you have to do is admit it, and it could be fine, but if you wait, like two days, then you might get into trouble.

Questions for Reflection (for parents):
1. Do you admit when you're wrong or when you've made a mistake to your kids?
2. Do you admit you're wrong to your partner/spouse?
3. How do you do it? Do you get angry, shameful, cry, passive-aggressive? Do you do it right away or does it take a while?
4. When you were a child, how did your parents handle it when they were wrong?
5. Do your children admit it when they are wrong?

Questions for Reflection (parents and children together):
1. Parent to child: When was the last time you remember that I was wrong or made a mistake about something?

2. How do you think I handled myself?
3. Do you think I should have done it differently? If yes, how?
4. What have you learned, if anything, from my mistake?
5. When I last corrected you, did I handle myself correctly?
6. If not, how could I have done it differently?
7. Did you feel loved in the middle of the consequences/discussion/struggle?
8. Is there anything left over from that time that we need to talk about now?

Divorce

My former husband and I decided to separate when Peyton was eight years old. It was a painful decision but one that I felt was the best for everyone in the long term. Fortunately, Peyton's father loves her and is a wonderful dad.

When it came time to tell her of our decision, she already knew it on some level. We had been arguing for some time and tried our best not to let it spill over into times when she was around us. But, "little people have big ears," as my mother always used to say. She hadn't missed much.

At a later point, I told her how I felt when my parents told me they were going to get a divorce. My parents sat down together with my sister and me on a weekend afternoon. I knew something was up, because the only time we all sat down together was at the dinner table. My mother did most of the talking. She told us they had tried to make their marriage work for a long time, but she and my father were going to get a divorce. I was shocked, but also not so shocked. I knew on some level too, but even at thirteen, I didn't really want to think about it as reality. It was the first and only time I ever saw my father cry. I didn't know what to do with the man who had been larger than life to me and who had presented himself as infallible, then see him suddenly lose it and admit he had failed.

Now facing my own divorce, it was crucial to me to have thought through what I wanted to tell my daughter so that she would have only the information which was appropriate for her and no more. I wanted to have worked through enough of my own feelings so they didn't spill over into this conversation. Her father felt the same way.

First, she needed to know that we both loved her. Secondly, she needed to know that she had done nothing wrong and was in no way responsible for our decision. This was a decision her father and I had made because our relationship wasn't working.

Both her father and I cried with her and apologized for how our choice would affect her. We told her we felt that even though this would be hard for a while, it would be better in the long run. Thirdly, we needed to let her know where her father would be moving. He had bought a condo near our house and would be moving there shortly. At the end of the conversation, we asked her if she wanted to go by and see it so that she would have as much security as possible, given the circumstances. She said she wanted to see it, so all three of us drove over to see it together. As strange as that may seem, that simple act let her know that her father and I could rise above our differences and the feelings of the moment and be there for her when she needed us.

For some couples, telling the children about their impending separation or divorce together as a unit is not an option. One mom says her former husband isn't good with "that kind of thing" and since she is a social worker, she told her children by herself. Explaining their decision in a way that her four and two-year-olds could understand was important to her. She explained, "Mom and Dad can't live together. If we stayed together, one of us would hurt the other one."

The amount of information and the way it is shared will differ with the age of the children. When children are in varied age groups and developmental stages, you may need to sit down at several different times to discuss the issue.

Visitation

Moving from an atmosphere of Mom or Dad being around every day, to one where they may split time every other weekend, is a huge transition for children. Even if there has been a lot of animosity before the separation, kids feel the stress of the big change happening in their lives.

When my sisters and I were getting ready to visit my father every other weekend, we invariably got into a huge fight before we went. The tension in the house was so high you could "cut it with a knife." We never knew what to expect when we went to his house and our fear manifested in arguments.

After a weekend away with the other parent, some children need to debrief about the time spent with him or her, and others do not. They may experience different boundaries or situations at the other parent's home. I generally wait until Peyton wants to talk about the areas of loss that come with divorce: the loss of the family unit as she knew it, the loss of the house in which we lived for most of her life, the loss of the dream of growing up as an intact family, the loss of her neighborhood and the traditions we had there.

Sometimes the loss children experience through divorce takes years to work through. One mom says her two children would cry every time they returned home after a weekend with their father. This lasted for two to three years after they separated. "I held them and listened to them, reassuring them our divorce had nothing to do with them; that we needed to do it for us." Now six years later, she says her children are okay. They talk regularly about how they are not the only ones who have divorced parents, and how different friends are dealing with it.

Talking about the other spouse

There is no doubt there is pain involved in divorce. How you talk about that pain will affect your children. Someone once said when you talk negatively about a child's other parent you are shaming part of their DNA. I believe that is true. A child will never feel the same way about your spouse as you do. Even if they have experienced pain in their relationship with their father or mother, it doesn't help them to add your pain/anger/grief to theirs. And if they haven't experienced that same pain, then you are only putting a wedge into *your* relationship with your child. Children will know they can't talk to you about certain things because either they don't want to upset you or because they feel loyal to you. In the end, they will form their own opinions about both of you ... the good and the bad. Don't add to it.

I was fortunate. After my parents' divorce, my mother never spoke negatively about my father or the reasons why they divorced until I was old enough to understand. The older I get, the more I realize how difficult my father was. My mother let me discover that truth on my own. She never used me as a "friend" to discuss all her frustrations and fears through the years. She talked to her peers for that.

Now as an adult, there are some things my mother could have told me earlier in my life, which might have opened up a dialogue about what makes for a healthy relationship. Because my father was such a private and mysterious person, I never really felt that I knew him or knew much about their relationship and how difficult it was for either of them. I didn't know that the rage I had experienced from my father was also directed at my mother in private and had begun before they were even married. I didn't know how lonely they both were for so many years. I didn't know that a partner is someone who treats you well and respects you. We just didn't talk about it. And because we didn't talk about it, I was left to fill in some of the blanks on my own, blaming my mother for the divorce and being angry with her throughout my teen years.

Saying too much also has its problems. Some parents make their children privy to any and every little thing in divorce negotiations out of their own pain and anger. The result can be immeasurable damage in the lives of the children, which may last well into adulthood. It's hard, when all of the drama of a divorce is in full swing, to keep your mouth shut in front of your children and talk about the anger, hurt, and frustration that prompted the divorce with your friends or a therapist. Taking the high road may not feel good in the moment, but your child will benefit both now and later. If your child is inundated with your feelings about the divorce, there is no room for them to discuss their loss and fears. The focus, then, becomes the parent and how she is coping versus the child. If you have found yourself guilty of this, you can change the tide. Stop talking in front of your children about the divorce and how the break-up is affecting you. Do it privately with friends, a therapist, or a support group.

Caring for yourself
One of my goals during the painful period of my divorce was to consistently take care of myself. I worked through my feelings of loss and pain on my own and with support of friends and family. I went on retreats which dealt specifically with loss and letting go of old patterns, so I could move on without bitterness. I wanted to continue to grow so I could model for my daughter that life goes on and I could be open to love again in my life. The result has been fairly amazing. I have found that staying friendly with your child's other parent benefits all involved.

Peyton's Point of View
Divorce was really hard for me because I really loved my old house, and I love my parents and just thinking about not having them together made me feel bad. If you're going through it, know that you're going to be okay because you'll always have both of them. It's not that they hate each other, it's

just that there were problems between them. This is hard to talk about.

Questions for Reflection:
1. Our family has gone through some big changes. What has been the most difficult for you?
2. What do you miss most about our life together?
3. Is there anything which is easier for you?
4. How are you talking about this with your friends?
5. Do you know anyone else whose parents are going through a divorce?
6. How are they handling it?
7. How are you making a home for yourself at your Mom or Dad's house?
8. Is there anything I can do to make this time in your life easier for you?

Step-parents and Step-kids

When I married, there was no way I could have been prepared to go from a family of one to a family of seven after saying some vows – no matter how much I thought I could. Yes, I married a man with five children. It was his third marriage and my first.

Over the ten years we were married, I am grateful for what I learned about being a step-parent to some wonderful human beings. But I also learned how selfish I was, how unprepared I was, and how much stress there can be in blended families for both partners. In the end, after trying extremely hard to make it work, there were ultimately too many factors that were against our relationship. Sadly, we aren't alone. Here are the statistics on divorce in the United States according to www.aboutdivorce.org:

Divorce after first marriages: 41-50%
Divorce after second marriages: 60-67%
Divorce after third marriages: 73-74%

Dating Again

What do you do when your former spouse starts dating or re-marries and suddenly someone else is having an influence in your child's life? Even if you're completely done emotionally, it can be tough to hear what "they" did together upon your child's return from a weekend at your ex's house. At some point, you must decide whether you trust your child's other parent to choose good influences then let go of the rest. Putting feelings aside and keeping up good communication on behalf of the child you share is essential. Even if painful, wouldn't you much rather keep the lines of communication open?

Your own dating can be a tricky thing, too. Since it's likely you will have to "kiss many frogs before you find your prince," keeping your dating life private until you are somewhat serious is important. Children don't need to be privy to every person you meet. It's not age appropriate for them to see that much into your private life and it's too hard for them to get attached to someone who may not be around several weeks later.

I remember my mother bringing home some men who my sisters and I thought were not worthy of her. My mother was still in her thirties when my parents divorced, with four daughters ranging from three to sixteen. One suitor was obviously interested in her way too much for our liking. My sister and I didn't like that he had a lot of wrinkles on his face. To show our dissatisfaction on one of their dates, we lobbed water balloons on my mother and her unsuspecting date from the second story window as they left the house. Poor Mom. It's no wonder she decided not to remarry until we were all out of the house.

What do you look for in a partner who will be good to your child/children? Certainly the things you looked for in a partner before you had children are still important: shared values, shared dreams, love of children, love and respect for you, among others. Is there a mutual respect between this person and your children? Do they "like" each other or is there constant conflict? How will they handle it when you disagree on how to handle an issue with the children? Will your child be a better person with him/her around?

I have a great role model in my brother-in-law who loves my niece as if she was his own biological child. He attends her soccer games, takes her to football games, to his parents' house, oversees homework, and loves her. He has earned the right to be heard by her because she knows he has her best interests at heart. He knows she has a father who loves her, but he is there for her too. Thanks, Pat.

Peyton's Point of View
Peyton decided to keep her feeling private on this topic.

Questions for Reflection:
If you find yourself in relationship and one or both of you have children, here are some basic questions that need to be sorted out as your relationship turns serious:
1. What expectations do you both have about the step-parent's role with the kids?
2. Are there unresolved feeling from the past (guilt, anger, resentment, fear) that are getting in the way of living in the present?
3. How will you handle disagreements?
4. Will you argue in front of the kids or behind closed doors?
5. How can the parent be supportive of the step-parent with the children?
6. How can the step-parent be supportive of the parent with the children?

7. Do you have the same values about education, money and kids, college and grad school expenses, adult children returning home to live, drinking and drugs, boyfriends/girlfriends visiting the house?
8. What will the involvement be of the children's mother/father in your lives?
9. How is power shared between the couple in regard to the children?

Pets

Before Peyton came into my life, I had a very neurotic, pure-bred Bichon Frise. I got him at a vulnerable point in my life and it was no accident that I chose him. He never "got" the house training idea. That means for the eight years I had him, he continued to poop and pee in the house, no matter how often or how long I walked him.

I struggled constantly over whether give him away, but I was stuck in guilt so badly that I couldn't part with him – until I adopted Peyton. The first day I introduced them to each other was right after we got home from Russia. I put Peyton down on the ground. She was still crawling and he was much smaller than she was. Moments later I heard screeching. I ran back into the room to find Bud on top of my little daughter, trying to dominate her (if you know what I mean!)

That was the last straw. I put an ad for Bud on the Internet and the next day he was adopted by a loving woman up in Boston.

Peyton loves to tell that story, but she was traumatized and terrified of dogs for quite some time. And her father is a veterinarian! She would go along with him when he did surgery and slowly but surely worked through her fear of being overpowered by animals.

When she was ready, her father and I decided she was old enough to take care of a dog. We went to several shelters and met many dogs over a period of days. We found out what kind of personality she wanted in a dog. Did she want to have a dog that played with her? Or did she want one that was very calm and docile – perhaps an older dog?

Finally, we found Max. Here's what she is willing to share about that encounter.

> PW: When I first saw him and when he first sat on my coat I knew he was the right one.
>
> SW: How?
>
> PW: Because I held him and he wrapped his little arms around me. He was so cute, remember?
>
> SW: Yes, I do, sweetie. What do you love most about him?
>
> PW: He comes in and licks my face. He's really a good friend, if you are lonely.
>
> SW: He's been there for you in some really hard times and given you lots of unconditional love.
>
> Peyton shakes her head.
>
> PW: And he's really good, because I dress him up in things like tutus.
>
> SW: He is a good sport. I can't think of another dog that would put up with something like that.
>
> PW: Yeah.
>
> SW: Do you tell him things you don't tell other people?
>
> PW: Yes…all the time.

In fact, Max has been the one to talk for her when things have been too hard to say. I might ask, "What does Max have to say about this?" Max usually has a lot to say that is very profound and sounds much like what might be on Peyton's mind.

In most families, pets become full members of that family. Dogs, cats, gerbils, ferrets, hamsters, rabbits, horses provide unconditional love and great fun for many years. They just seem to know what a family needs and provide it. In our house, Max has been a great sport too, wearing wigs and skunk, pumpkin, reindeer and ballet costumes. He dances and bounces back no matter what we do. We love you, Max.

In her book *What Animals Can Teach Us about Spirituality,* animal behaviorist and therapist Diana Guerrero tells why animals touch our souls so deeply.

> *"Animals remain bound to the Spirit and so do not follow any religion or spiritual practices. Because of that direct connection many of us lack, animals can link us to the Divine in new ways. In essence, animals can help us in our personal and spiritual growth, and compel us to pursue a connection to Spirit without the need for a religious or denominational approach. Some people search their entire lives for such a connection. Learning how to relate to animals can be a first step to recognizing how to unite with your spirit."*
>
> Excerpt from What Animals Can Teach Us about Spirituality: Inspiring Lessons
> from Wild and Tame Creatures 2003 by Diana Guerrero (Woodstock, VT: SkyLight
> Paths Publishing)

That's true, isn't it? She goes on to say how different animals "embody ideal traits" and serve as "good examples of right action" which, in turn, help lead us humans in the way of Spirit. According to Guerrero, dogs, for example, embody loyalty and show us that the quality of bringing out the best in another is a trait worthy of emulating.

Once I felt annoyed with our dog Max, who was whining. He was sitting at the bottom of our stairs with his head and ears alert, waiting for Peyton to wake up and get out of bed so he could welcome her to a new day of play. My annoyance receded. Max's loyalty is stunning. If only I could be as welcoming of everyone in my life, everyday, all the time.

Not every family should have pets. Animals require time, energy and commitment over the long haul. Some families have schedules which are just too full to give a pet the time it needs. Peyton has more to say on that point.

Peyton's Point of View

If you get a pet, you need to really want it. If you don't really want it, you may not play with it, and rely on your parents to take care of it. You could also be mean to it, and that's not good. I used to be scared of dogs. They were too big and they barked too loud. But one day that changed ... when I met my baby, Max.

Questions for Reflection:
Think about each of the pets who have been part of your family.

1. What did it take for you to get your pet?
2. What do you love most about your pet?
3. What has each pet contributed to your family?
4. How is your family different/better/worse because of each pet?
5. If your pet could say something out loud to you, what would it be?
6. What secrets does your pet know about your family?
7. What has your pet taught you?
8. What's the biggest gift your pet has given you?
9. If you could tell your pet something right now, what would it be?
10. If your pet was a person, what type of person would he/she be?

Having Fun: How About Another Whipped Cream Fight?

When I was little, Saturday mornings were full of chores around the house. It usually took me around three hours to get them all done. The message I got was never make a mess, because I would probably have to clean it up. "If you have fun, it means more work," and "Good little girls don't make a mess," were ideas I internalized. So it's no wonder that I grew up a "good little girl" who wasn't much fun to be around sometimes!

For much of my daughter's early childhood, I reacted when she played freely, with an overpowering fear that she would "mess things up." This oversized energy was fueled by an ancient feeling that her "mess" would leave me with more work to do, or I would somehow be in trouble. It was irrational, but nevertheless real. The result was I squelched much of her "just fun" because I had no clue what having fun looked or felt like. The idea of totally "letting go" and playing for an extended period of time had been lost to me long ago.

I realized I needed to change. I decided that those old patterns were not what I wanted to pass on to my daughter. Who wants to be around a stick in the mud?

I spent some concentrated energy on healing the feelings from the past, examining where those feelings had come from and why I felt so inhibited to just "let go" and play. After all, what would be the worst thing that could happen if we got lost in ecstatic play for a long period of time? I found that old habits die hard; I was rusty around the edges for a while. Here's a conversation Peyton and I had after a doctor's visit:

> SW: Dr. Brennan isn't as relaxed as Dr. Kemper, huh?
>
> PW: What do you mean?
>
> SW: Well, he's a bit more of a stick in the mud.

PW: Well…

SW: Is that what I'm like sometimes, a stick in the mud?

PW: YES! Like *tonight*!

We laughed.

SW: I'm sorry, honey. I've really been grouchy tonight.
    I'm really tired.

PW: (jokingly) You make me feel like a small bug!

We laughed again.

SW: What can I do so you don't feel that way?

PW: How about laughing more or doing some crazy
    dancing.

SW: I just did tonight!

PW: Yeah, but I don't mean the kind that embarrasses me!

More laughter.

She later came up to me and gave me a big hug.

Sigh. I was forgiven for being a stick in the mud.

One day I decided to see what totally letting go of my "stick in the mud-ness" was like. I surprised Peyton after dinner that evening by sneaking a can of whipped cream out of the refrigerator and then spraying it … right in her face and then all over her body!

The shock on her face was priceless. Then she screamed, "OH NO YOU DIDN'T!" She immediately grabbed the can and went after me, spraying it all over me. We laughed until our sides hurt – you know, those gut-busting, side-splitting laughs where you cry and almost wet your pants.

Then of course we took off our clothes and put them in the washing machine and cleaned up the floor!

Then there was the Disney Cruise. I decided to let loose and volunteered for the hypnotist's show on board. I became Hannah Montana for a few minutes on stage, lip-syncing and dancing to a song I didn't know. It shocked my daughter that I would act so out of character. We laughed over how silly I must have looked up there.

Try This:
Suggestions for a laughing home:
1. Lighten up! Laugh at yourself!
2. When you are in the middle of a difficult time, let loose and do something nutty.
3. Read the comics together.
4. Watch an age-appropriate comedy show on television together.
5. At dinner each night, share one thing which was funny that day.
6. Smile, smile, smile!

Did you Know?
Did you know that the first Sunday of May is "World Laughter Day?" An article in *Ode: For Intelligent Optimists* relates the tradition which started in 1998 in Mumbai, India. According to the World Laughter Day website (www.worldlaughterday.org) the goal of the day is to "change the world in a peaceful and positive way." Why not check out the website and start practicing now?

Peyton's Point of View
My favorite thing to do is play outside with my friends. I love to play lots of games. I use my imagination, play basketball, go on the swings, play stick war with the other kids, and football. With my family I play usually by going on vacations.

If you don't think your life is not that much fun, you can make it fun. It's not hard. It's all a matter of your perspective.

Questions for Reflection:
1. What is something that you could do with your child that

would totally shock him/her to see you doing?

2. Do you see yourself as someone who likes to have fun, either with your children or with other adults?
3. What is the craziest thing your mother or father has ever done? (Both parent and child answer.)
4. What do you wish your parents would do more?
5. How did your parents react to free play? (Parent may want to share this with their child.)
6. Talk about a time when you both shared one of those gut-busting laughs together?
7. What was that like for your relationship?
8. What keeps you from doing that more often?

I Have Loved You for a Long Time

How did your child/children come into your life? Birth, adoption, surrogacy, death of their birth parents? The meeting of two souls here on this earth through the parent/child bond is sacred. The journey in getting to that bond takes many forms. Some easy, and some long and arduous.

For many women, the experience of pregnancy is joyous. They love the idea of their baby growing and developing inside them. They take special care of their bodies to prepare for the day of birth. After nine months of preparation, they welcome their newborn with loving arms into an environment which is ready and waiting for her.

For some women, their road to being a parent is fraught with difficulty. Many deal with infertility. Plagued with the idea that giving birth should be the most natural thing on earth, they suffer when their experience is different. Injections, hormone pills, scheduled sex, doctor visits, and treatments fill the lives of many hopeful parents. For some the end result is a baby. Others end up having to find another way to fulfill the dream of creating a family.

Some parents meet their child through either domestic or international adoption. Time and energy is spent making application, finding the right birth mother, the right situation before the little child is welcomed home. One mom with two adopted daughters thinks of it this way: "My children were out there waiting for me to come and find them." Her job was to look until she found them. One happened to be in Vietnam and the other in China.

The journey through the welcoming of a new life into a family is profound. As you come into this world, the experience you have carries with it a deep imprint which affects the rest of your life on a soul level. What was the situation into which you were born? Were you welcomed or did your arrival present problems for your parents? Were you loved or was your presence a burden? Whatever your experience, you have the opportunity to give welcome to your own little one, now.

First words, first crawl, first steps, and early personality traits are all bits of information which can help a child fill in their idea of who they are. Sharing those stories with them is an important part of self identity as they grow up.

Letting your child know over and over again in your words as well as your actions that you love them unconditionally, and have since their very beginnings is a gift that has profound ramifications. A child who doesn't receive that message from a significant adult in his or her life, will grow up to be a wounded adult.

As we walk along with our children, we will do things which will test or damage that bond. We have a much better chance of mending it if our kids know without question that we love them. Frederick Douglass once said, "It's easier to raise healthy boys than to heal wounded men." What are the ways you show your children you love them?

Every once in a while Peyton wants to hear about the beginnings of our life together. Some of the details will remain private between the two of us, but here is what we have agreed to share.

After a year of fertility treatments, I found out at age 38 that I was unable to have children because I was on the verge of menopause. For me, it wasn't a huge thing because I had always considered international adoption.

From the moment I saw the video of my little girl who was then seven months old in a Russian orphanage; I knew … I just knew, that she was mine. It was the end of January 2000. With a face on the dream, I began to make specific preparations to bring my daughter home. I started singing to her whenever I thought of her. At that time the Disney version of *Tarzan* had come out and the lyrics of the soundtrack, such as *You'll Be in My Heart* and *Two Worlds* spoke right to the issue of adoption. I sang these songs over and over.

The day finally came to go get her. I wrote this journal entry on the very day of our meeting in Moscow, Russia in June 2000:

My Dearest Peyton,

It's 1 am on the morning we are to meet and I'm so excited, I can't sleep! So much has gone into this coming day. I just finished gathering together the gifts from all of the people who have lovingly cared for you over these months until now. I am so grateful for everything they have done for you…and very soon, it will be my turn! I can't wait.

I also brought you some toys, some to give you now and some to give you when you come to live with me at the hotel here. I want to help you grow and learn. We have so many wonderful days and years ahead of us, my darling daughter.

There are many people who also can't wait to meet you. They've been praying for you, as I have been over these months. I wish I could take you home with me tomorrow, but I'm not able to. I will be holding you close in my heart every day, though. On July 3, less than a month, we will be together all of the time.

God has wonderful things in store for us. Right now I open my heart to you in a new way, as we meet face to face. May our bonding be deep, fast and permanent.

I love you,

Mom   (It feels so good to say that)

In spite of being up for most of the night in anticipation, I got up bright and early that day. The whole thing seemed a bit surreal. I asked my Russian translator to capture our first meeting on tape.

It was magical. Peyton had been in the infirmary due to a fever from cutting teeth. The caregiver brought her to me. She was an angel with bright blue eyes and white blonde hair. I couldn't take my eyes off of her. I was so present for that moment, fully alive and intentional in my words and actions. My heart was completely open to this little girl. I started talking softly and then singing lullabies to her. I also made up some of my own songs that I whispered to her.

She had some developmental delays due to having been in an institution, but within ten minutes of our meeting, we were touching each other's faces and cooing to each other. The bonding had begun.

This was the truest love I had ever known. There was no doubt in my mind that this was my daughter. She had just been born on the other side of the world. It just took me a while to get to her.

Peyton loves to hear that story especially in the mornings when she needs some cuddle time to be reassured that everything is okay. Sometimes I will stop and spend a minute or two, literally, to look at her face. I tell her, "I just want to study everything about your face. I want to take it all in." It goes well beyond words. She is usually very quiet. She loves it.

Peyton's Point of View
It is important for kids to know what happened when they were little. Like what did they do best? What was it like the first time they crawled? Their first walk? When they first used the toilet! I wanted to know what I was like and if I'm the same as I am now. Was I helpful? Did I love chocolate? (Thanks, Dad for giving me my first chocolate bar!) It was cool to learn that I was very helpful to other children who were crying and I made friends easily. I also taught other little children how to crawl.

Questions for Reflection (for Mom)
If by birth:
1. When did you first know you were pregnant?
2. How was your pregnancy?
3. What were your hopes for your child before birth?
4. How did you prepare for his/her arrival? (What things did you buy, was there a shower given, did you sing to him/her or plan special things as you awaited the arrival?)
5. What were the circumstances of the birth of your child?
6. How did you feel when you first saw your child?
7. What was your first encounter with each other like?
8. Was anyone else in the room? What was their reaction?
9. Describe your first weeks together.
10. How much of this have you told your child?

If by adoption:
1. What was the journey like for you and your child to find each other?
2. What did it take for you to actually get to him/her?
3. What was your first meeting like?
4. What was your first thought when you saw your child?
5. How quickly did you begin to bond?
6. Were there other people there? Who were they and what were they doing?
7. What kind of care had he/she received before you got there?
8. What if anything do you know about your child's birthparents?
9. If adopted internationally, how do you feel about your child's country of origin?
10. How do you help your child appreciate their roots?

When Mommy or Daddy Drinks Too Much

Eight years before I adopted Peyton, I stopped drinking alcohol. I also took a course to become an alcoholism counselor. Because I met with so many families in the church who had issues with alcohol, I felt I needed some additional training to assist them.

Long before I stopped my own drinking, I attended meetings to figure out the effects of my father's drinking on my life. The sudden mood swings and unpredictable behavior, the rigidity of the household, the lack of real intimacy, and my father's inability to deal with our feelings were all parts of his alcoholism that left a deep imprint on me. It was hard to label what I experienced from him as alcoholism, though, because my father always worked in high level jobs. I never saw him falling down drunk. I never smelled alcohol on his breath. After my parent's divorce, Dad's drinking escalated. He died at the age of 57 from Larynx Cancer, the cause of which is most often drinking and smoking.

Years later, as I tried to pierce through the isolation and loneliness that I felt as a child, and which still plagued me as an adult, I came to understand that alcoholism is a family disease. That means that even though one person may be the drinker, each person in the family is affected and needs help to recover for the family to become whole. The good news is families *can* recover. There is hope, but it begins with recognizing there is a problem, talking about it and getting help.

One of the first things I heard when I walked into Al-Anon (a twelve-step group for friends and family members of an alcoholic) and ACOA (Adult Children of Alcoholics) meetings was I was powerless not only over my father's alcoholism but also over him. I would never be able to make him change. The only person I could change was myself.

This slogan was repeated at each meeting:
- You didn't cause it
- You can't control it
- You can't cure it

While it would be a long time before I could even begin to understand what that meant, it sank in deeply as truth. I was relieved that someone was speaking a language which spoke to my heart. In those groups I learned that alcoholism is a disease, much like any other disease. The drinker is ill and that illness affects him physically, mentally, and spiritually. As the alcoholic recovers those pieces begin to be restored, but the family may still be left in shambles. Anger, fear, repression, denial, and many forms of abuse may have all been operative within the family for years. The untangling of that web may also take a long time.

Unfortunately, many people in families where there is addiction or dysfunction of any kind may develop and internalize shame as a way to operate in the world. In his book, *Healing the Shame That Binds*

You, John Bradshaw describes the difference between healthy shame and what he calls "toxic shame" in developmental terms:

> *"Toxic shame, the shame that binds you, is experienced as the all-pervasive sense that I am flawed and defective as a human being. Toxic shame is no longer an emotion that signals our limits, it is a state of being, a core identity."*

And caregivers have a huge role in our development of healthy or toxic shame:

> *"If a child can be protected by firm but compassionate limits; if he can explore, test and have tantrums without the caregiver's withdrawal of love…then the child can develop a healthy sense of shame…healthy shame signals us that we are not omnipotent."*

Bradshaw says that if children are brought up in shame-based environments where addiction occurs, they are not able to develop a healthy sense of self and emotional life. What was a healthy sense of shame turns to a toxic form of shame.

And the cycle continues. Those who were raised by shame-based parents may grow up and marry others who are shame-based and they may have children who become shame-based. The cycle can keep repeating until someone is conscious enough to do the work it takes to rebuild and heal his inner life. The good news is it can be done, by the grace of God.

Peyton's Point of View

If that happens to you, you should tell your parents to stop and they shouldn't be drinking when a kid's there. Maybe you're feeling sad if your parents are acting crazy and can't control themselves. It's going to be okay. Why don't you tell them when they're not drinking, that you don't like it when they drink like that. Maybe you're thinking when you're older you won't be able to control yourself when you drink.

Questions for Reflection (for parents and children):
1. Do you think Mom or Dad drinks too much?
2. How does it make you feel?
3. What do you experience when he/she drinks?
4. Is there any specific time when he/she was drinking that you want to talk about?
5. Do you feel safe when he/she drinks?
6. What do you wish you could say to him/her?
7. Do you think they would hear you?
8. What do you need right now?
9. Would it be helpful to go and talk about it with someone else?
10. Is there something you need to say to me as a parent?

Questions for Reflection (for parents):
1. Do you think you or your spouse has a drinking problem?
2. Have you ever tried to stop and couldn't?
3. Does alcoholism or drug addiction run in your family, either through your parents or grandparents?
4. Has alcohol ever been connected with instances where you have had trouble with the law?
5. Have you ever suffered injuries as a result of behavior when drinking?
6. Do you suffer from depression?
7. How is alcohol handled in your house around your children?
8. Does anyone (other children) else drink in your household?

Alateen groups are available for children ages 12-20. To find a local group, go to www.al-anon.org. If you or a loved one has a drinking problem and wants help, go to www.aa.org or call your local chapter of Alcoholics Anonymous.

Responsibilities

How much responsibility do you give your child around the house? Some parents give a lot, others very little. How ever your household operates, your child needs to learn responsibility for herself at some point – unless you are hoping that she will live with you and depend on you for everything for the rest of her life. (For some, that may sound like a grand idea!)

In my elementary-school years, my sister and I had loads of chores to do every week: cleaning the bathrooms; vacuuming the floors; mopping the kitchen floor; cleaning our rooms; polishing the piano, the kitchen chairs and the leather car seats; raking the leaves outside and disposing of them. We also set the table nightly and washed the dishes after dinner. While the list may have been a bit excessive, our parents' intent was to prepare us to take care of ourselves and instill a sense of responsibility. I am grateful for their care and concern.

Children need to know that being part of a family means helping to keep it running well. Participation in household chores builds self-esteem and identity as part of a group. But just how much responsibility is appropriate for different ages? Some households list all the chores and divide them up according to the number of people and the age of each to be fair. Sometimes families choose to rotate the chores so everyone gets an opportunity to do each task. Whatever the case, it is wise to discuss expectations so everyone is on the same page and acknowledgement and appreciation is given on a regular basis.

Responsibility for self care:
At what age do you let your children take responsibility for their appearance? Should parents still be dressing their fourth graders? Some would say yes, others, emphatically no! If you need to hold onto a particular area of responsibility, ask yourself why. What is your motivation? Is making sure your child wears perfectly ironed

matching clothes a reflection of her or of you? If you are still making your child's lunch in the fifth grade, is it because you want to make sure the five food groups are represented, or because you will feel like a failure as a parent if you don't? (If your motivation is to show love and care for your child who was up late the night before studying, then that's a different matter.) If your response is, as one parent said, "It's just easier for me to do it," consider that may be true in the short term, but it won't be in the long term. When your son or daughter grows up, he or she won't be able to manage for themselves, and *that* would mean you haven't done your job.

In our house, I was often frustrated with the daily struggle of getting Peyton up and ready for school. Like in many other households, our routine became tiresome very quickly. All too often, our mornings ended up in some kind of struggle just to get my daughter to the bus on time. I knew it had to stop because I didn't want her going off to school mad, and I didn't want to start my day that way either.

After I attended a parenting course designed to give children more autonomy, we sat down together and made a list of things she would be responsible for each evening before bed, and in the morning before school.

Here's a sample list from when Peyton was in third grade:

In afternoon and evening:
- Do homework
- Go through backpack for any notes sent home
- Care for pets
- Clean up dinner dishes
- Take a shower
- Get out clothes for the next day
- Get sports equipment or other needs for after-school together for the next day (including notes and transportation schedules)
- Make lunch for the next day (older elementary)

- Brush teeth
- Comb hair
- Set alarm
- Pray (for some families)

In the morning before school:
- Make bed
- Take care of pets
- Get dressed
- Get backpack together (put lunch inside and get any gloves, mittens, and hat together)
- Make breakfast (for some older elementary)
- Brush teeth
- Kiss parents good-bye!

The lists were clear and visible. Some parents use a similar listing and attach a reward system to indicate how well the list is followed. We tried that and then decided it wasn't necessary for our household. Peyton was doing a good job and liked that I wasn't nagging her as much as before. She was doing it all without any prompting. The reward was the satisfaction of taking care of herself.

Peyton's Point of View
I have to take care of my dog, feed, and play with him. I have to do the dishes. I have to make my bed, my lunch. Those are not really chores, they're just things I do around the house every day. It's okay. I actually like making my lunch because then I can pick anything I want. If my mom did everything for me I would probably just be sleeping all the time, wake up, go to school. I wouldn't know how to do things to help me grow up. It's actually kind of fun, because you feel good when you finish it all. You feel good about yourself. Even if you try it once, you can feel good that at least you tried. Sometimes I don't want to do the things, but I just remember that I would be without my lunch at school. It's my routine.

Questions for Reflection:
1. What is the atmosphere like in your house in the mornings?
2. What responsibilities could be given over to your child? (both answer)
3. (To your child) Do you know what is expected of you in your house on a regular basis?

When Families Share More Than One Faith Tradition or Culture

Someone said the heart doesn't decide with whom it falls in love. So the fact that people of differing faith traditions, or no tradition at all, intermarry isn't as rare as it was a few decades ago. I have come across many families where the parents of the household come from two different faith tradition: Jewish/Christian couples (both Catholic and Protestant), Buddhist/Christian couples, Christian/Hindu couples, couples who are both Christian but different denominations, and those like my parents, atheist/evangelical Christian.

Each couple decides how they will deal with their backgrounds in different ways depending on the commitment they have to their tradition. Those decisions can become more cemented as children arrive. I have seen some creative configurations.
Some have elected to raise all the children in the tradition of the parent most committed to their faith. That means the children attend the religious education of that faith, attend worship, and observe religious holidays. The children identify themselves as being members of that faith.

Others have chosen to expose the children to both traditions and when they come of age, the children choose which one they will follow. If parents are really open to whatever the child decides, this can be interesting. Sometimes it ends up being a melding of the two religions. Clergy from some faiths discourage intermarriage for this very reason, because they feel it waters down their traditions.

Still another family I know of raised one son in the mother's faith (Christianity) and their other son in the father's faith (Judaism). This arrangement seemed to work very well. They all attended the Holy observances of both faiths as an entire family.

Whatever the situation, it is important for the couple to have the discussion about how they will raise their children, preferably before they marry. Regardless of how the family lives out their religious tradition, the important thing is to let your children be aware of their heritage so they can appreciate it.

Peyton's Point of View
Church is important to me because it makes me feel this is the place I am supposed to be. I get to do fun things in Sunday School and sometimes I get to speak in front of the whole church. All the adults and kids love you, especially if you've been there for so long, and it's important for you to see them. I like the traditions in the church too, like the Christmas pageant, and picnics and the Christmas Fair, and church dinners when everybody gets together.

Questions for Reflection (for parents):
1. What faith issues did you and your spouse face when you decided to marry?
2. Did you have the support of your parents and your faith communities?
3. Did you talk about how you would raise your children?
4. Are you or your spouse more committed to their tradition?
5. Are you able to keep some of the traditions of both? Which ones?

Questions for Reflection (for children and parents together):
1. How do you feel about your parents being from different religious backgrounds?
2. What traditions do you like from each?
3. Do you have any curiosity about the other faith tradition?

2

School and Learning

"Checking In" After School

Here are some ways we get around the dreaded "fine" or "good" response to "How was school today?" I now ask questions that are more open-ended and require more than a one word response.

When Peyton told me I wasn't asking the right questions, she said she wanted to be asked something like, "What did you learn in social studies today?" (And then she told me that she didn't take Social Studies! Okay, I finally got it. I was working a bit too hard.)

One friend told me her husband tried a different strategy. When he came home from work, he would simply tell his two daughters, "You have sixty seconds, and only sixty seconds to tell me how school was today." When I first heard that idea, I thought it might convey a lack of caring; that he only *wanted* to hear sixty seconds worth of information. But in reality his nightly question made his girls cram all of the important information into that one minute. They made a sort of game out of it. Then at a later point, he would ask more about something that they had said during that minute update.

Some kids just need "down time" after being at school all day. Many adults don't want to come home and talk about everything that went on at the office either. I have learned to let a little time lapse and possibly approach the conversation at the dinner table. After establishing a new kind of rapport as a result of this exercise, I am now also more trusting that if she has something she really needs to talk about she will tell me.

Peyton's Point of View
Sometimes I know kids don't talk to their parents after school because they're embarrassed, or maybe they don't want to get in trouble for something that happened. Maybe they want to keep a secret, or they just don't want to say anything.

But I think kids should talk to their parents, because something really bad could have happened and maybe someone got hurt or something and no one knows about it. Maybe something good happened and their parents can congratulate them. Parents need to know about stuff because they're your parents! Parents just want to know because they want to make sure everything is alright.

Questions for Reflection:
1. What was the best thing that happened at school today?
2. What was the worst thing that happened at school today?
3. What did you learn today that you didn't know yesterday?
4. What was the most interesting thing that happened at school today?
5. What was the funniest thing that happened today?
6. If you could live today over, what would be the same/different?

Homework

Depending on the grade of your child, the amount of time she spends on nightly homework will vary. The task of the parent of an elementary-school aged child is to help – that's right, help, not *do* – with the child's homework, so he can develop good study habits which will carry him through the school age years.

My sister has taught gifted students in kindergarten, third, fifth and now fourth grades for the last decade. We laugh together when I hear about some of the things parents have said to her. "We spent three hours on the homework last night. I didn't understand that math that you gave my child. It was way too hard." Okay, what is wrong with that response? Here's what my sister said: "First of all, *we* should not be doing your child's homework. I gave clear instructions in class, but if Johnny doesn't understand and if he has tried for an hour or so and can't get it, then you can sign off on it and he can ask me the next day. Homework should not be frustrating. Parents should be soothing. Let your children be mad at me, not at you."

What a concept! The problem for many parents is that they are overachievers. They cannot stand to think that homework will be turned in unfinished or less than perfect. They put pressure on the child to do it perfectly or else there is struggle. That scenario has certainly happened in my house.

What is your experience – and your child's experience – of this nightly routine? Is it a struggle or does it go smoothly? How long does it typically take to complete? In order to help develop proper study habits and make it as positive an experience as possible, here are some factors to consider:

A. YOUR CHILD'S EMOTIONAL STATE:

- Does your child need a break after school (45 minutes or so) or does he like to get right to studying and get through quickly?

- What kind of snack do you give him? Something without excessive sugar will help him concentrate better. Fruit, nuts, or popcorn are good ideas.
- Other considerations are extra-curricular activities; does she need to have dinner or a rest before beginning homework?

B. THE RIGHT ENVIRONMENT THAT WILL FOSTER CONCENTRATION ACCORDING TO YOUR CHILD'S LEARNING STYLE:

- Your child needs a quiet place.
- Consistency is important; preferably the same place and time each day.
- There should be sufficient light.
- Does he have a flat, clear surface upon which to write, with no toys or gadgets sitting around?
- Ensure there are few if any distractions: no TV, iPods, preferably no other siblings or pets around.
- Make necessary materials available such as paper, pencils, eraser, pens, dictionary. (My sister keeps this all in a "homework box" ready to go.)

For some households this set-up may be impossible due to the amount of space available, or the needs of siblings at the same time, but you get the idea. Children learn best when they can concentrate. Study time should not be a time requiring multi-tasking skills.

C. THE RIGHT METHODS OF STUDYING:

I turn to teachers for this one. Some suggest:
- Focus on one task at a time; for example, your child can do all of her math first, or social studies, instead of skipping around to different subjects.
- Figure out what gives your child the best results. For some, it is doing the easiest assignment first, versus the longest. This

way the child feels some sense of accomplishment before taking on something more difficult or time consuming.

Time Management

One of the most important skills children need to learn during the later elementary-school years is time management. Children start getting assignments for both individual and group projects by the third or fourth grade. Those assignments only increase in middle school, so it is better to learn how to manage several things at one time while the pressure is lower.

If parents aren't good at time management themselves, this may be a challenge. Too often, good time management skills are not used and parents end up staying up late with their child the night before the project is due. The result is the parent ends up doing much of the work. This doesn't help anyone in the long run. Even worse, your help may erode your child's self-esteem, because, while he may get praise for how great his project is, he knows it's not his work.

Try This:
Children under age eleven don't have the maturity to plan things ahead of time without some help. Here are some ideas to get you going when he/she is assigned a special project:

- Sit down together and discuss the scope of the project soon after it is assigned.
- If your child has any questions he needs to ask the teacher, get them answered immediately.
- Look at a calendar and determine together what family obligations, sports, or other activities will be happening before the project is due, and plan around them.
- Plan together how much needs to be done each week in order to finish the project with plenty of time for review.
- Make allowances for creative thinking needed for the project.

- If household items are needed, gather them together in one spot.
- If materials need to be bought, purchase them together.
- If your child asks for help, keep it to a minimum and encourage him to find a way to work it out, or ask the teacher for help. (This may be uncomfortable at first, but it will pay off in the long run. Let him come up with the creative ideas. He's smart!)
- When your child is finished, celebrate together!

Peyton's Point of View

Homework? Not my favorite. I just want to go outside and play. It's usually pretty easy, though. Even though I don't really like it, I still do it, because then I don't have to go to my teacher and tell her I didn't do it. Sometimes I race through it so I can go out. I feel tempted because the kids in the neighborhood are all younger and they don't have as much work, and I hear them having a fun time. But if you don't do it, you're not going to understand it and you'll pay for it later. One thing that helps me if I'm having a hard time or getting bored is to break it up my work and read in between, then I can get back to it.

Questions for Reflection (together):
1. Which homework subjects are easiest for you? Why?
2. Which homework subjects are most difficult for you? Why?
3. What do you like about math (or science or social studies, etc.)?
4. What would you like to learn about in science (or social studies, etc.)?
5. How can I help you feel more successful in your studies and at school?
6. What can I as a parent do to help you concentrate better? Do you need more time, a quieter environment, or study habits hints?
7. Do you feel that your questions are being answered in school?

8. How do you think your teacher would describe your work habits? Do you agree?
9. Are your after-school activities getting in the way of your studies? Do we need to make any adjustments?
10. How do you feel about the work you do at home?
11. Is there anything more we need to talk about now?

Friends Are Really Important

Friends *are* really important, at any age. The memories they share can last a lifetime. In a girl's life, the choices of friends she makes can be reflective of who she is and how she feels about herself, both positively and negatively.

Groups of friends start forming very early in elementary school. For girls, some groups include the "smart ones," the "popular ones," the "athletic ones," and the "tomboys," as well as those who don't fit into any labeled group, or who don't want to be in a group. There may be groups of students with similar ethnic or religious backgrounds. Parents need keep an eye on who their child is getting to know and which groups she is a part of to monitor her development.

Boys mainly form groups around similar interests, like sports, for example. Team sports start early in life and are great places to form friendships which can last for years. Parents have an opportunity at games to get to see their sons in action among their friends and meet their parents. For boys who are not interested in sports, other interests such as music or art may provide friend groups.

Children can act mean at an early age. Think back to a time when you had a falling out with a friend in elementary school. Your world felt like it was tumbling down. For girls, if it goes to the extreme, it can be the "mean girl" syndrome. It eventually can lead to bullying. These behaviors start much earlier these days than I remember from my own childhood. The next chapter goes into bullying much more extensively. Here, we're talking about friends having a falling-out over what can be a minor reason.

Here's a conversation Peyton and I had about her friend:

> SW: Do you want to have a play date with Krystal today?
>
> PW: I don't like her anymore.
>
> SW: Did something happen recently to make you feel that way?
>
> PW: No, she's really mean to me and she ignores me on the playground.
>
> SW: Wow, you have been friends for so long. I wonder if she knows if you feel this way?
>
> PW: I don't care. I hate her.
>
> SW: Honey, you sound hurt. Hate is a very strong word.
>
> PW: I don't want to play with her anymore.
>
> SW: I understand. I don't always like everyone either.

Helping your child through the sometimes rocky roads of young friendships is a hugely important task. They're working out who they are and how they are out in the world of friendships, which can be wonderful yet prickly too. Being there to listen to their concerns and provide support as well as keeping disagreements "right-sized" are key roles for parents.

Here is the continuation of our previous conversation:

> SW: I wonder if things will be different on another day. Do you think something might be happening in her life to make her act this way right now?
>
> PW: I don't know.
>
> SW: What can you imagine might make someone act nice

one day and really mean another day?

PW: Maybe they're having a bad day or they had an argument with their brother.

SW: Hmmm.

PW: Maybe she feels bad.

SW: Maybe so. You've always been really good at being sensitive to what other people are feeling. Do you think you might be able to ask her how she's doing?

PW: I don't know.

SW: What could you say to her? Do you want to practice what it might sound like? One thing that is helpful to me is to say something like "When you do this...I feel hurt or something like that" instead of "you are mean."

Peyton agreed to a role play about the situation:

PW: Hi Krystal

Krystal: (played by me) Hi... (Nonchalantly looking away.)

PW: You've seemed a little angry lately. Is everything alright?

Krystal/SW: What are you talking about?

PW: Well, the other day on the playground you were mean to me.

SW: Whoops! Remember "I feel..."

PW: The other day on the playground I felt hurt when you said you didn't want to play with me and then you went off with Katy and Chrissie.

Krystal/SW: Sorry

PW: That's okay. Do you want to play now?

Krystal/SW: Sure.

While the reason for the hurtful interaction may not have surfaced in that role play, Peyton learned some tools and was able to practice owning her feelings with someone who has hurt her. It also helped build trust with me, who was willing to walk through it with her. Role plays gives children a guide to how they may deal with future conversations – even between parent and child.

When we were reading together one night, we read about a situation which sparked a conversation about what was happening in Peyton's life. Over the last three days, two of Peyton's friends weren't talking to a third friend. A similar situation in the book provided an opening to talk about what was going on.

SW: Wow, have you ever had that happen?

PW: No…

SW: What do you think she did to make them not talk to her for so long?

PW: I don't know.

SW: If that ever happened to you, what would you do?

PW: I would go up to them and say, 'Hey guys, why are you being so silly?'

SW: And what if they ignored you?

PW: I'd say, 'Can we talk about it? What's wrong? Let's be friends.'

SW: You know what I like about how you did that?

PW: What?

SW: You didn't take it personally. You tried to use a sense of humor to get them talking, and you realized that their reaction may have more to do with them than with you. What if you knew you had

done something really wrong and that's why they
hadn't talked to you?

PW: Then I would say, 'Hey guys, I'm really, really
sorry. Please forgive me and I forgive you. Let's be
friends, okay?'

Children change as they grow up. Some friendships end like
the seasons. Knowing if and when it is time to walk away from
someone who is being mean is also important. As a parent, you
can be there to listen to and help gauge if the interaction seems to
be taking a permanent turn or if the friend is "just having a bad
day." In any case, encouraging your child to know they always have
a choice in any relationship will be a lesson for life.

What if your child is befriending someone you feel is unsuit-
able? As his parent, you can see trouble coming down the road
if your son continues to hang out with this boy or girl. Talk
with your child to understand what he likes about this person.
Be clear about what behavior you expect and what is and is
not appropriate.

Peyton's Point of View
As far as kicking someone out of a group, I don't think people
should do that. It's not very nice. If that's happened to you, it's going
to be okay. You'll find new friends, even better friends. It's not fun
to be sitting alone at the lunch table or have no friends at recess. I
never liked it. When that happened, I tried to find more friends. I
have a lot of friends, but I usually play with certain ones. When I
found myself alone, I played with other friends that I hadn't played
with in a while. It made me feel better that I didn't need those other
friends right then. Another thing that's hard is when you feel left
out with two other friends. It makes me feel that I'm not important.
But maybe they're just having a bad day. If I wait, a lot of my friends
come back. They say they're sorry they were having a hard time and

I ask them, "It's okay, what was it about? Are you okay?" They tell me what was happening and I let it go. Then I ask, "Do you want to go and play?" and we start playing again.

Questions for Reflection:
1. Have any of your friends ever been mean to you?
2. Have you ever found yourself being mean to someone else?
3. Have you understood what was going on?
4. How have you handled it?
5. If you haven't said anything, what would you like to say to the person/people?
6. Why do you think friends are sometimes mean?
7. Do you think you could talk to your friends about this before it happens? How would you approach them?
8. Do you have some friendships which have ended? How did you both handle it?

Bullying: Always stick up for the kid everyone picks on– not only because it's the right thing to do, but because someday it may be you.

Back in the middle of my fifth grade year, my family and I moved from Westchester County, just north of New York City, to North Carolina. It was a hard move for me because I loved my school and friends in the quaint New York suburb of Chappaqua. But I was also eager to make new friends at my new school.

On my first day, I went out to the playground during recess. A group of kids, both boys and girls, whom I had sized up to be the "cool" kids in the class, stood around me in a closed circle. They started chanting, "Yankee, go home!" They

continued for what seemed an eternity until it finally oc-
curred to me to walk out of the circle. Feeling totally dejected,
I walked over to the side where two girls were waiting for me.
"Just ignore them. We're really glad you're here," they said.
Those two girls became instant friends and remained my
friends for many years.

I don't remember if I told my parents about it, even though it was
excruciating for me. I internalized that experience to mean "You
don't belong." That feeling would haunt me for many years, until I
learned as an adult to let it go.

Fast forward to one afternoon when I picked up Peyton from
school. She and I saw a fifth grade boy sitting on the side of the
sidewalk, crying. Peyton and I went to see if he was okay. It turns
out the boy had been kicked by another boy after school, and not
for the first time. It was clear to me that it wasn't only his leg which
was bruised; it was his spirit too. The bullying had left him feeling
hopeless and bad about himself.

The boy accepted our invitation for a ride home, because he said
he was afraid the other boy would be waiting up the street to
continue his attack. We confronted the bully as we drove by. He
looked at me and said, "Whatever."

The next day I called the principal of the school who intervened in
the situation. After talking with the boys and their parents, it was
discovered that the bullying had been going on for some time. She
said that if we hadn't said anything, the situation could have gone
on much longer and gotten much worse.

The point in telling the story is that Peyton saw all of this and witnessed the effects of bullying first hand. She saw the importance of
telling an adult and what a difference it can make.

Before you start thinking "Wow, that was so great," fast forward another year. We were at our town pool and a girl a year older than Peyton, and much larger, wanted to play with her and her friend. All seemed to be going well until Peyton's friend left and the older girl and Peyton remained. I could tell this girl was trying to control Peyton.

We had already decided to eat dinner at the pool. The girl announced that she would come over with us to eat, although she had just eaten a sandwich. When we were in line, she asked Peyton if she could share her dinner. (She was pushing my buttons big time.) I said, "This is going to be Peyton's dinner, and she needs to eat it, or else I'm going to hear her say, 'I'm so hungry' five minutes after she's eaten." The girl backed off and said, "Okay, I have some snacks." While we waited for the food to cook, I left for a moment. When I returned, the girl was drinking a soda. Somewhere in the back of my mind, it occurred to me that this was strange, since she didn't have money with her and had no soda when I left – but I said nothing. Then a boy came up and started looking around. The girl piped up, "Somebody came and must have thrown your soda away. This one's mine … yeah, I had a Sierra Mist." I glanced at Peyton who was staring down at the ground. Clearly something was up, but for some reason, I was not fully present and again, didn't say anything although I didn't feel comfortable with what was going on.

After the girl left to go home, I asked Peyton if the girl had taken the boy's drink, and she shook her head yes while looking at the ground. "She peer pressured me, mom, asking me if I dared her to drink it. What was I supposed to do?" We came upon the dejected boy waiting at the counter. And even though I bought him a drink, I still felt badly about how it had all gone down. I had missed a teachable moment when I hadn't confronted the situation.

Everyone lost in that moment. No one felt good about themselves or about how the situation ended. And the girl is probably continuing to act similarly with others and not realizing the impact she is making.

PRACTICAL APPLICATION:

Feel something, say something. If an interaction feels bad to you, chances are, it is. Talk to someone about what happened so you can understand how you can respond differently next time.

A few days later, Peyton and I were reading a book together about a boy bully. The boy was at a boarding school and was facing a peer honor court. They were confronting him, trying to figure out how he had become a bully. It seems that he had been jealous ever since his twin brother and sister were born and all the attention started going to them. Ever since that time, he had treated younger kids badly.

We stopped reading and I asked Peyton if she had any idea why the girl at the pool had acted like such a bully. We talked together about how we had watched her ride away all alone and wondered if she was alone a lot.

PW: I always see her alone, Mom.

SW: That must be very lonely and sad for her. I didn't handle that very well the other day. I should have stopped it. How could we both have done that differently?

PW: I could have said to her, 'You peer-pressured me'

SW: What if either of us had just said, 'I feel uncomfort-able with what's going on.'

PW: I don't want to play with her ever again, but she may want to play with me.

SW: But what if you could be *in* your body and say, 'I don't feel comfortable with what happened the other day, and I don't want to play with you.' How would that be?

She shook her head.

SW: It doesn't help *her* to let her keeping doing this to people. How many people do you think have felt the way we're feeling right now, and she had no idea?

PW: (Speaking through tears) Mom, I don't feel good that I let myself be peer-pressured and didn't say anything.

SW: You didn't do anything wrong, honey. You didn't make her take that boy's drink. We both learned something from this and we can do it differently next time.

PRACTICAL APPLICATION:

Bullying never takes place in a vacuum. There's usually some reason why someone acts this way. Understanding the person brings compassion and the power to intervene.

Bullying occurs all the time. The above examples may seem obvious, but sometimes the bullying is just enough to make someone feel bad, but not enough to make them think telling someone will help.

Here's an example from a teacher friend. Every day she has her fifth grade students write in their school journals. One day she noticed an odd entry in Arman's journal. (Arman, born in India, was short with a slight build.) "When we were outside today, Stuart was not nice," Arman wrote. (Stuart is bigger than Arman and they are best friends.) When the teacher asked him about it, Arman said, "I'm not strong enough sometimes." He told how Stuart pushed him out of line at times, and shoved him around. The teacher saw that Arman looked uncomfortable and reluctant. He also told her that Stuart was acting similarly with another boy, who was also small. That boy, Mark, had not said anything.

PRACTICAL APPLICATION:

Many people are unable to stop a bully without help. Find someone who can help.

The teacher asked Mark what had happened. "Nothing," he said. She told Mark what she had heard Stuart had done to him. "That's not true," he pleaded. The teacher insisted. "Stuart pushed you in line and made you get out of the way. Did you tell anyone?" she asked. Mark hung his head. "No, because nothing is going to be done," he said.

She talked to Stuart, who defended himself by saying, "We were both going for the ball, and I just got there first and he got pushed out of the way." She confronted him. "It is clear you are angry. I don't know why you are angry." "I don't know why either," he said sheepishly. She told Stuart of the possible consequences of his bullying, such as calling his parents, going to the Guidance Counselor, or having him write an essay on why he did those things. And then she looked at him and said matter-of-factly, "Today is the last day this is going to happen."

From that day forward, the teacher said the turnaround in Stuart was remarkable. He was still angry sometimes, but he began to let his vulnerability show. In his yearbook at the end of the year, she wrote, "Huge Heart and Mush." The teacher was able to see through what was really happening and intervene in those boys' lives.

PRACTICAL APPLICATION:

With the right help, bullies can change and so can those who are bullied.

Bullying can be a bit trickier for boys in our culture, who are taught from a very early age to be tough and not to "be a baby." Many young boys would never have said anything, like Arman, and they would have most likely grown up getting picked on by every person who was literally and figuratively bigger than they are *for the rest of their lives*.

Every time you stand up for yourself and say what you feel to any person, big or small, it is an estimable act. It makes a statement about how you feel about yourself and how you relate in the world. We need to help children (our own and others') stand up for themselves so they will continue to develop those skills throughout their lifetimes.

Try This:
Sometimes the most profound conversations begin with you sharing with your children a time when you acted in a less than kind way to someone else. Then you can ask them, "Can you think of a time when you made fun of someone else in front of others? How did it make you feel?"

Peyton's Point of View
If you're being bullied, it means that maybe the bully has problems, maybe at their house. Maybe their parents talk to them in that way and it makes them feel bad. They're just taking their anger and putting it out on you. I don't think that's good. Just be strong for yourself and ask them a couple of questions to find out

if they are feeling bad at their house. I know how hard it is to stand up for yourself sometimes.

If you're bullying others, why are you being mean to kids? It's not very nice to be mean to them. Just because something happened in your family, you don't have to show everybody. You're just going to be the person who everyone doesn't like, and wants to get away from. You won't have any friends.

Questions for Reflection:
1. What would you have done if you had seen the boy who was kicked on the side of the road?
2. How would you have handled the girl who took the soda?
3. Would you have told the teacher if someone was consistently shoving or pushing you around? Why or why not?
4. What do you think was going on inside the lives of each of those bullies?
5. Do you know any bullies at school?
6. How do you feel about them?
7. How do other children act around them?
8. How does it make you feel when you see someone acting mean to another child?
9. Did any adult ever step in to help?
10. Why don't you think any adult was told?
11. If you were in a situation where someone was bullying you, what would you do?

Inquisitive minds

The educational system is different now from when the baby-boom generation was in school. I have memories of writing down exactly what the teacher said only to spit it back out for a test. While that style certainly worked for some, it did little to pique interest and curiosity. I was so worried about memorizing facts that I had little energy left for wondering "what if?"

Much of that seems to have changed, and thankfully so. Along with the whole "question authority" movement of the 1960's, adults are raising their children in a more inquisitive time. Many schools are now places which give children an opportunity to wonder and figure out who they are, how they fit into the world, and why things work the way they do. In subjects such as science and history, literature and social studies, teachers hope to ignite enough curiosity to pique a student's interest for more.

Curiosity feeds that desire to learn, to look beyond the obvious and explore new horizons. Great inventors, educators, scientists, and explorers have all been sparked by curiosity. Just think: what if Lonnie Johnson hadn't been curious in his senior year in high school – we never would have had the world-famous water gun, the Supersoaker! Or how about Earle Dickson who was curious about how to keep a bandage on his wife's cuts? Thanks to him, we have Band-Aids! Or James West, the famous African-American inventor who brought us microphones. He says this of his insatiable curiosity during his youth, "If I had a screwdriver and a pair of pliers, anything that could be opened was in danger. I had this need to know what was inside." (source: By Kids For Kids, www.bkfk.com)

Try This:

Ways to Spark Curious Investigations
- In the Kitchen: Some children love to make their own concoctions in the kitchen -- ketchup in cola mixed with hot pepper powder, and other juicy concoctions. This is hard for me because of my hang up of "But it will get dirty!" At times I have been able to put that aside and let my daughter create. Give your child the responsibility for clean up, and let her loose!
- Outdoor Exploration: There's so much in nature to spark

curiosity. Digging for worms, catching lightning bugs on a warm night, going fishing and hiking, or looking at mushrooms, algae, or mosses are all fertile laboratories for asking, "Why?"

- Science Experiments: There are tons of websites that have great ideas for safe science experiments your child can do at home, with parental supervision, of course. On www.sciencebob.com, young scientists can learn how to make their own volcanoes, balloon rockets, orbs levitate, slime, and a small rocket out of a film canister.

Curiosity in Relationships

Being curious can also help with relationships. Sometimes, we sit back and wonder what is happening in someone's life to make him/her act a certain way. I once heard this story: a woman got on a train and noticed a man with his three children. The children were out of control, getting up out of their seats, hitting each other, and running around. The father, meanwhile, looked off into the distance, not even noticing the chaos his children were causing. Fed up with the noise, the woman finally spoke up and asked the man if he needed help with his kids. The dazed man seemed startled at first, and then said, "Oh I'm so sorry, I just got word that my wife died and we're coming back from the hospital."

That information certainly changed how the woman saw the situation, from feeling annoyed and judgmental to compassionate. That's what having a sense of curiosity can do.

Keeping a sense of curiosity about other people also helps you detach from the actions of a person who may be doing something hurtful or pushing one of your emotional buttons. Being curious gives you a sort of "pause" button in your response before reacting to someone's behavior. It gives you the opportunity to respond with empathy.

Barriers to Developing Curiosity

Children need time and space to foster curiosity. Speeding through life at 100 miles an hour with every moment of the day filled with activity makes it difficult to have the mental space to ask what is going on in the moment. Many children as well as parents are so "busy" (even with "great" activities), that time for reflection is lost. Parents pick up their kids from school then rush from soccer to baseball to dance class to tutoring and who knows what else. Hectic schedules leave children and parents exhausted and depleted. They may be unable to take a step back from life and just wonder.

Even if the fast pace slows down, the mind has become addicted to the adrenalin rush and needs more to continue. It's no wonder there has been an exponential rise in video gaming over the last decade. They keep adrenalin-hungry brains fed. Many households have consoles going for hours each day, and that too can zap curiosity about life. Sure, much of the gaming provides opportunities for problem solving and strategic thinking; but connection with other humans, other than on a "virtual level," is severely diminished.

Parents are guilty, too. Constant input from news channels, cell phones, Blackberries or email keeps us from interacting with people right next to us. How did we ever survive before all of this technology?

One day on *Oprah*, families were asked to "de-tox" from all electronics for a week. I was stunned and saddened as I watched how difficult it was not only for the children, but for the adults to disengage from watching TV, playing video games or using computers for a week. However, those who were brave enough to go through it, and live to tell what happened, said they wouldn't go back to the way things were. Members of the two families actually awakened to each other. It was as if a veil was taken from their eyes. They looked more alive, and seemed happier and healthier. Conversation among them was full of life, versus the dulled interactions they exhibited before the experiment. I'm not so sure the children agreed, but the parents were given a major wake-up call. Good job, Oprah!

I have seen that same phenomenon on a smaller scale in our house with Nintendo DS and television. For awhile, anytime we would get in the car, Peyton would want to have her DS with us so she could play. The days of just sitting in the back seat, talking or just being quiet and thinking seemed to have passed. Then the DS was lost. All of a sudden we had our own forced "de-tox" and had to deal with, "What am I going to do for twenty minutes while we're driving?" Goodness, twenty whole minutes. Fortunately, we've always loved music and we sing regularly to songs on the radio and on CD's. I wonder sometimes what people think as we drive by with songs blaring. Who cares? It's one way we can connect together.

Try This:
Take the Challenge! How about taking the plunge? See if you and your family can stay off of television, computers and all other electronics for even a day. Or even a week. Have accountability with another family. Then talk about what it was like.

Peyton's Point of View
If you're not curious about stuff, it may make you dull and boring. I'm curious about what makes my cotton candy machine work. I'm also curious about worms. Where are they and how did they get there? So, I dig and I search the web to find out. Sometimes I find out and sometimes I don't.

Questions for Reflection:
1. What would you do if you had no access to any electronics for a whole week? No television, computer, video games, cell phones – what would it feel like? Take a few minutes to imagine what you might do during that week instead.
2. Can you remember what life was like before electronics came into your household life?

3. Do you know anyone who is very curious? What are they curious about?
4. What is something you want to know more about? Why?
5. What makes you curious about it?
6. Have you ever had an idea that you think could change the world?

Imagination

Imagination is the ability to see what we can't see with our eyes. It helps us experience life through another dimension. It can affect how we view life. Imagination plays a part in whether we are an optimist or a pessimist, in whether we are hopeful or full of dread. Imagination is also utilized in the ability to maintain faith.

We use this gift in some form every day. Our imaginations are called upon when we read books or go to the movies which take us into another world. Some careers are even built on using it, such as marketing, long-range planning, problem solving, inventing, visioning. The world of "make-believe" or fantasy is an essential aspect of imagination especially for children. When children play, they use it. (See movie reviews of *Bridge to Terabithia* and *Mr. Magorium's Magic Emporium* in Chapter Six) However, as we reach adolescence the love of fantasy is quickly pounded out of our lives, seen as something frivolous and only for the young. Unless young people are encouraged to continue to use their imaginations in play and fantasy by the adults around them, they will lose an extremely important skill. Fortunately, attempts at keeping fantasy alive are rewarded at the box office. Great examples can be found in science fiction and popular series based on classic books such as J.R.R. Tolkien's *The Lord of the Rings*, or C.S. Lewis' *The Chronicles of Narnia: The Lion, the Witch and the Wardrobe*.

Long ago, before people wrote down stories, they passed on their stories through oral tradition. The idea of sitting around a campfire or fireplace, hearing about how their ancestors lived, how something got its name, or about area legends was an integral part of community life. We've lost some of that in modern times. We've become more and more self-centered as a society. We have lost our sense of wonder and appreciation of all that has gone before us. So many people have accomplished great things to allow us to do what we do and be who we are.

Much like curiosity, imagination needs precious time and space to thrive. Acting, drawing, painting, pretending, exploring, storytelling, meditating, game playing are all activities which engage the imagination.

Try This:
There are many games you can play that will let you know what other people are thinking about, and which make a great jumping off place for conversations. Here are a few we've used.

- Traveling Stories: Start a story where you make up a line and another person adds the next line. Continue the story until you come to a natural conclusion. We played this game on a car trip with a friend one time. My friend started the story about a monster and a headless creature that scared the entire town. The story twisted and turned with each person's addition, and I was interested to see that Peyton's additions were short and positive. When my friend added some particularly scary elements, Peyton's additions turned them into hopeful situations. In our story, the two scary creatures ended up becoming friends and went to a costume party where everyone was dressed up like them and they all started getting to know each other. Others at the party recognized that there was no reason to be scared.

This game can also be done over email with friends or family members to help with creative writing skills.

- I've got a secret: That was the name of a television show a long time ago. You can play this with two or more people. One person is chosen to think of a secret and writes it down on a piece of paper. It can be something that happened to them, something they did that was embarrassing, an achievement, or something they like or would like to do. Then they give a clue by saying, "The secret concerns something that happened to me."(Or whatever the topic is.) Then the other person or people take turns guessing what it is. Make sure the children and adults both share secrets so both sides find out a secret about the other. It equals the playing field.

- Mind Travel: If you could go anywhere in the world, imaginary or not, where would it be and how could you get there? You could make a food dish from that place; go on the Internet and research about the country; imagine what the children do for fun in that country; find out if your child can get a pen pal there; if there is another language involved, your child could learn some words in that language.

At our house, we have placemats at the dinner table that are world maps. We use them as a jumping-off place to dream about where we'd like to go someday. We wonder aloud about what life might be like there. We also talk about current events that are happening in that area of the world in an age appropriate way.

- We used to love to lie down and look up at the clouds. Even something as simple as this can give you a lot of information about what's going on inside your child's mind.

SW: What do you think is above the clouds?

PW: All of the people who have died are there.

SW: What do you think they would want to say to you if they could?

PW: How's everything down there?

SW: What would you say in return?

PW: Oh, everything is just fine, but we sure do miss you a lot.

You might continue by asking: Where do you think that cloud is going? How big is space? How long do you think it takes to get there?

- Charades is a wonderful game to play which immediately transports you into the world of imagination. For younger children up to age six, "Kids on Stage" (by University Games) is an excellent version of the game. "Guessures" (By Hasbro Games) is a version for older kids.
- Writing in a journal is an inexpensive way to encourage imagination. Parents and children can write together in their journals daily or a few times a week. You can take turns coming up with a prompt. For example, "If you had a magic wand, what would you do?" Then write for an agreed-upon length. After a few entries, share them together. All you need is a notebook and a pen or pencil!

Peyton's Point of View

If you want to have fun, you need imagination. If you don't have it, you may be all glum. I use it when I go with my dad to work if I get bored. If you have imagination, you can imagine things like there's a field of beautiful flowers, or your dog's there, or that you're babysitting or that your friends are there.

Questions for Reflection:

1. If you could live in another time in history, when would it be and why?
2. If your pet could talk to you, what would he or she say?
3. If you had a magic carpet and could ride anywhere, where would you go and who would you take with you?
4. If you were out on a deserted island and could only take four things with you, what would they be and why?
5. If you could wave your magic wand over your family right now, what changes would you make?
6. If you had a million dollars what would you do with it and why?
7. If you met someone from another country, what would you ask them?

8. If you suddenly found an alien creature living among your toys, what would you do?
9. If you had super powers, how would you use them? Add your own!

Dealing with Learning Disabilities

Your child is growing, but you've been noticing for a while that she doesn't understand what she's learning in school in the same way that other children do. You're concerned. You wonder, "Does my child have a learning disability?" According to www.helpguide.org:

> "A learning disability, or learning disorder, is not a problem with intelligence. Learning disorders are caused by a difference in the brain that affects how information is received, processed, or communicated. Children and adults with learning disabilities have trouble processing sensory information because they see, hear, and understand things differently."
>
> Excerpted with permission from "Learning Disabilities in Children: Learning Disability Symptoms, Types, and Testing." Visit (http://www.helpguide.org/mental/learning_disabilities. htm) to see the full article with links to related articles. ©Helpguide.org. All rights reserved

We live in a time when parents, school personnel and doctors are more aware of the learning issues children may face. But parents are still the best advocates for their children. If you have concerns, talk to a professional. Request testing be done in your local school district or through your pediatrician. Get the answers you need.

One mom, who also happens to be a teacher, noticed her preschool aged son wasn't expressing what he needed on a regular basis. His teacher also noticed a similar behavior. They tested the boy for speech and language issues. After investigation, he was diagnosed with Tourettes' Syndrome, a neuropsychiatric disorder as well as an auditory processing disorder. Both Mom and Dad did their research as to how they could best advocate for their son, which included making directions sheets for different tasks and taking advantage of support systems. Mom said the support systems helped her recognize that she was having a hard time stepping back to see how her son was compensating to fit in at school.

In our case, I was especially watchful because Peyton had been in an orphanage for the first year of her life. I was told that for every three months a child is in an institution, he or she generally may be a month delayed in developmental skills. Pediatricians watch this carefully and refer their patients for early intervention services. This enables children to be up to speed by school age. Peyton did qualify for speech therapy and occupational therapy. After six months of speech therapy she was at an age-appropriate level. Since she was enrolled in Montessori pre-school, they were able to address her gross motor skills without additional services.

As Peyton developed, I noticed she was easily distracted and hyperactive during reading. She'd often put her head down on the desk during homework, and wrote words off the page. I knew she had an eye that "wandered;" an eye specialist had told us to put a patch on her strong eye, which did no good. Fortunately a friend's daughter had just completed vision therapy and suggested I get her tested. It turned out that Peyton's eyes weren't tracking together which meant she wasn't able to find her place on the page again if she looked away. She was also seeing with double vision, but since that had always been the case, she didn't know any different. That translated to behavioral issues too. After five months of treatment, she was able to bring her eyes together and focus on her work. She immediately began to excel in reading and her behavioral issues subsided. There is still so much to be discovered about learning disorders, but the field has grown tremendously and research continues. There are many resources for parents if you have concerns over your child's development.

Try This:
There are books and helpful websites on different learning disorders. But here are some things one teacher with special education training suggests as action steps:

- Make sure your child's teachers and his friends' parents are aware of his diagnosis.
- Make every situation a learning situation. For example, ask, "What can you do differently next time so this doesn't happen again?"
- Normalize the diagnosis. Research your child's particular disability and find famous people who have the same thing and how they have dealt with it.
- Let the child be his own advocate and stand up for himself.
- Play up their strengths.
- For families who have children with different needs, parents may want to split their time so each child gets one-on-one time with a parent. For example, if your son has learning issues which require undivided attention, dad may read with him one night, while mom reads with your daughter.

Peyton's Point of View
When I was younger, I didn't know I had issues with my eyes, because it was all I knew. My eyes would go out, one this way and another the other way. People would tell me. Now I can see better. I feel better that people don't have to look at me and go "What's happening with your eyes?" But as far as anything going on with a person, you don't need to feel bad about it because you're still the same person with or without it, you just have a little problem that you need help with. And you can get extra help to help yourself. You're still like everybody else.

Questions for Reflection (for parents):
1. Do you have any concerns about your child's learning abilities? What are they?
2. Does your child behave similarly to others of his age? If

not, what is different about your child?
3. Have you spoken to your child's teacher, friends, or pediatrician about your concerns?
4. How would you answer this: If my child could just_____, he would do better in school.
5. What is one thing you could do today that could ease your mind or answer a question you have about your child's behavior/needs?

Question for Reflection (with children):
(please note that depending on the issue, children may or may not be able to answer these questions)
1. Do you have any frustrations when it comes to your school work or anything at home?
2. What are they?
3. What's difficult for you to do? What's easy?
4. How would you answer this: If I could just_____, I would feel better about myself.
5. Have you noticed if you do things differently than others at school? If so, how?
6. Do you feel understood by me, your siblings, your teachers, your fellow classmates?
7. Can you tell me how I can let you know that I understand what is going on for you?

Team Sports

Soccer, baseball, basketball, softball, swimming, hockey, lacrosse, martial arts … they fill the lives of many families beginning in elementary school. Town and parochial leagues get kids active and give them the fabulous benefits of working together. In addition to building physical strength, sports teach sharing, togetherness, problem-solving skills, assertiveness, strategy, responsibility, discipline, and respect. They encourage self-confidence, and teach important lessons on how to win and lose.

Sports activities are ways some kids bond with their parents, too. One mom of three says her husband plays hockey. Her daughter took up the sport when she was in elementary school to have "special" time with dad. The other two children joined in also. Good thing everyone is on board, because mom says she is out four nights a week transporting them all to practices and games!

That brings us to some of the challenges. What do you do if most of your free time on the weekend is spent on the field or on the court, for games and practices? It can take a toll physically, emotionally and spiritually on each person as well as the family unit. Coordinating schedules and making room for children and parents to have "down time," as well as time to interact as a family, is essential.

And then there's this challenge. Were you ever the last one chosen when teams were picked? As the pool of people got smaller, you probably just wanted to slither away until your name was called. Ugh. My heart sinks just thinking about it, yet it happens every day. If a child is resilient and has the inner fortitude to withstand that type of vulnerability, he's fortunate. Others may need help to know that situation is not about rejection.

Still another challenge can be the parents themselves. One coach of elementary students says, "It's surprising, once to the bell rings, to see who changes. Courtesy goes out the window." We all know what he's talking about – parents who cross the line from cheering to obnoxious behavior. They tend to be the ones who live through their kids on the court/field/rink and ruin it for everyone else. Still, in most cases kids and parents have wonderful experiences through team sports. If everyone can keep it all in the right perspective they can be phenomenal laboratories for learning.

Peyton's Point of View
I like basketball, but boys can be rough! The best thing is, I can play!

If you make a shot or something, you feel good about yourself. But other times, it's hard when you are all the way open and people don't even notice you. All they want to do is throw it to their best friends. I just tell myself, maybe I'll get it next time. And then I practice so that I can get better and beat the boys' butts! Yes! (laugh)

Questions for Reflection:
1. How do you feel when you're on the field, the court, the track or the rink?
2. What does doing your best require from you?
3. Is it easier to give your all as an individual athlete or as part of a team?
4. What does it mean to you to be a team member?
5. What lesson have you learned from being part of the team?
6. How important is it to you to be a good team player?
7. What makes a good or bad coach?
8. How does playing as a team member help you *off* the field?
9. How do you feel about your parents' involvement?

Winning and Losing

The saying goes, "It's not whether you win or lose. It's how you play the game." But I've been to my share of little league games to know that saying doesn't hold true for all players, coaches and parents. When parents overreact in a game what does that teach their children?

> SW: Is it important for you to win? I asked Peyton
> one day.
>
> PW: No…

Well, that's not entirely true. Put a game of Yahtzee out in front of us and we go at it, for several games. And she is good. More than once she has rolled not just one, but several Yahtzees (that's a roll where all five die are the same number) in one game. She felt on top of the world. "People, people, the dice are hot – why are we turning on the stove?" she once screamed after rolling her third Yahtzee!

I learned to be competitive early on in life. Winning was important to me, but it seemed elusive when I was around adults. My father loved to play Monopoly when my sister and I were in elementary school. He made us stay up until the wee hours of the morning until he was winning before he let us go to bed. I have had a hard time shaking that one. So it has been hard for me to let my daughter win in board games. Actually, Peyton is as competitive as I am about certain things, so I have to keep an eye on how emotions are running when we're shooting hoops or playing a board game. Since I know she can win honestly, I am not one to "let her win" just because she's younger. Okay, I've still got issues here. I'm sure by being so intense, I'm giving her issues for therapy in the future! Ugh…

The point is, there are lessons to be learned in winning as well as in losing fairly. It's life. And it also *is* how you play the game that matters.

Peyton's Point of View
Winning and losing is not important. Who cares if you don't win? If you want to win all the time, you're just being selfish. It's just a game. Just try your best and if you don't win, tell the other person, "Good job." Be supportive.

Questions for Reflection:
1. How do you feel when you win at a game?
2. How do you feel when you lose at a game?
3. What lessons are there to be learned either way?
4. Have you ever "let" someone win a game? Why or why not?
5. Has someone ever let YOU win a game?
6. What is your favorite game and why?

3

Money and Things

Teaching children financial literacy brings self-esteem and empowers them to function as responsible participants in the world. I am grateful to my parents who taught me how to handle money early in my life. They felt that allowances shouldn't be tied to chores around the house. You did those because you were part of the family. Allowances were given for the sole purpose of teaching about money.

By age nine, I was receiving not only a small regular allowance, but also a clothing allowance. I was responsible for purchasing all of my clothes, including coats and shoes, and had to keep track of the monthly receipts for an accounting showing how I had spent my money. That was a way of keeping checks and balances on my spending and to make sure I didn't blow the whole wad of $40, which was a bundle back in 1968, on some funky piece of clothing, or records! Barefoot, but rockin'!

My parents also had to deal with a budding entrepreneur. When I was in nursery school and watching *Romper Room*, I saw a commercial for hosting a circus in your backyard to benefit research for Muscular Dystrophy. Many parents would have squashed such a scheme from a five-year-old, but mine let me go for it and never discouraged me. And, by the way, we had an audience of eight people beyond our family!

During later childhood years, I made and marketed candles and appliquéd skirts. My older sister and I designed and ran a summer camp for my younger sister's friends. All of this by the age of twelve. Needless to say, my neighbors were generous souls as they saw me come around with samples of the latest thing I had made, take my orders and deliver the goods.

Hoping to instill a sense of financial literacy in my daughter from an early age, I read different books about children and money. Robert Kiyosaki's *Rich Dad, Poor Dad* was my first stop. Even better was Kiyosaki's board game called *Cash Flow For Children* which Peyton and I have played, and played, and played. The game is a cousin to Monopoly in that it shows children the value of passive income, or money that works *for* you, in such investments as rental real estate, businesses, and stocks with dividends. It also teaches the impact of debt. For example, purchases that are made with credit cards are subtracted from your salary each time you go around the board. Other debts, such as mortgages and other loans, are paid each go-round as well.

A player wins when her passive income is greater than her expenses each month. It's a great way to teach about finances and gives ideas on how children can start to create wealth while they are still young. The genius is that since there can be multiple winners, there is no competition as to who gets the most money. There is enough for everyone. Money management is the goal.

Most children are taught early and learn by example what is expected of them – grow up and get a job. The reality is that few children will be able to support themselves on the starting salaries they will earn even after a college education. This game gets them in to the pattern of thinking outside the box early on in their lives.

When my daughter was in the first grade, I started giving her $4 per week in allowance. The rules were that she had to save a dollar of it, give away a dollar, and spend the other two on whatever she wanted. She actually divides the money into different containers. I have increased it every year as she learns to handle her money responsibly. At the beginning of fifth grade, however, she is still receiving only $6 per week.

Giving Money

It's important to develop a habit of giving money, as well as spending it and saving it. Some children may already be earning money in their elementary-school years. How are they handling it?

Since we started the giving, saving and spending routine, Peyton has amazed me with her ideas of how to stretch a dollar through giving. She has thought of creative outlets such as buying toothbrushes for the homeless of New York City, giving a $10 scholarship to our town's summer camp program for a student in need, and buying canned goods for the local food drive.

The idea of giving back has prompted her generous spirit in larger ways too. A few weeks after the Tsunami which devastated parts of southern Asia, my daughter (then a first-grader) and I talked about what she could do to help. She decided to run a coffee and cocoa stand. She made posters with another little girl and we negotiated with the owners of a local gas station to use a corner of their parking lot to sell our drinks. The gas station owners generously donated cups and coffee, as well as her first $50. We supplied the coffee fixings and cocoa and hot water. As the two girls stood outside on a cold January afternoon, yelling out "Tsu-lami Relief," money started pouring in. They raised over $125 in just an hour and a half.

The next week when we took it to the local chapter of the American Red Cross, Peyton beamed with pride as she handed over the money.

Children can be quite creative in their giving. One day at a church where I worked, the Director of Children's Ministries gave each child two dollars and an assignment. They had to see how far they could make that two dollars go by giving it away. The idea was modeled on the Biblical parable of the workers who were given money/talent and then later asked how they spent it. One buried it, another spent it foolishly but the third man invested it. The result? It grew exponentially. The moral: use the all of the gifts (money and talents) you have been given for the greatest good.

After a couple of weeks, it was amazing to see how the children followed the example in the parable. Some had just sat on it, others spent it on "stuff," but a couple had invested it and it had grown. One girl bought a dog collar for the new puppy in the neighborhood. She knew this would not only make the puppy safer, but would give relief to the neighbor. Another family of three girls pooled their money. They bought cookie mixes and made cookies. They then practiced their musical instruments and went to a local retirement home and entertained with cookies and a concert! Now that's what I'm talking about!

No matter how much or how little you have, you can always practice giving. I'll never forget a man from Kenya whom I met during my first few days in seminary. His name was Mbabu. He had come to the United States by himself, leaving his family back in his homeland because he could not afford to bring them. He was obviously missing them, knowing it would be at least four years of study until he received his PhD.

A friend and I met Mbabu in his small apartment one afternoon. He offered us a spread of tea and cookies, a Kenyan tradition of hospitality. I said, "Mbabu, this is too much! This is so expensive for you." He looked back and said, "My dear Shannon, I give when I have a little and I give when I have a lot."

No matter how much or how little someone has to give, the important thing is that they give something of their time, energy, or talents to others. Teaching your child this principle not only builds self-esteem and values, but it creates habits which will help them be long-term contributors to the communities in which they live.

Peyton's Point of View
Giving is important because there are people out there who are needy, and if we don't help, a lot of people could die. It feels really good to give because every time you give or do something for someone else, they will be helped.

Questions for Reflection:
1. What are some ways you contribute to others in the world right now?
2. Where or to whom would you give money, if you could?
3. Is there any way to make your money multiply to help more people?
4. What is a cause you would like to help over a long period of time?
5. Do you think you could help inspire others to give what they have too?

6. Do you think it is important to give to others?
7. What difference do you think your gift will make?
8. Do you feel any different when you have given something to someone?

(See the review in Chapter Six of the movie *The Ultimate Gift*.)

Saving Money

After the financial downturn in 2008, more people in the United States started saving their money. This is encouraging news as children are now witnessing a changing trend in the ways their parents are spending and saving. If that trend continues, our children may benefit exponentially. The miracle of compounded interest (interest paid on previously earned interest) can work in their favor if they begin the habit of saving now.

Here's an example of how a small amount of money can grow over time. Susie has $100 and never adds anything to it for twenty years. If she invests it at 3% compounded annually she'll have $180.60 at the end of twenty years; if she invests that same $100 at 5%, she'll have $265.33 in the same amount of time; and if she invests $100 at 7%? She'll almost quadruple her investment at $386.97. Just think what can happen if Susie added *any* amount to that $100!

What are the saving habits in your household? Teaching children at a young age to save for something long-term or for a relatively big purchase helps them learn about patience and delayed gratification. It brings a sense of accomplishment once they finally make a purchase they've been waiting for over a period of time.

A while back, Peyton and I started searching the Internet to look for various stocks that she might like to buy. She wanted to use the "saving part" of her allowance that she had accumulated, combined with some birthday money. Going on the principle of "buying what you know," we talked about the companies that she sees every day and those that make the products she uses. We narrowed our discussion down to a few stocks that were solid and she picked one or two and bought a share of each.

One of the things we do together monthly is check on the Internet to see how her stocks are doing. Has the stock increased or decreased in value? She knows that she has a part in saving for her future and she feels good about contributing.

Peyton's Point of View
It's a little hard to save money. You get may want a toy but you've spent all the money you have to spend. All you have left is your savings, but you still want that toy. But saving money is good, because when you're older and you need a car, or something big, you can go to your account and all of the money you've saved when you were a child is there. You'll have a lot of money then.

Questions for Reflection:
1. What do you think about saving money?
2. Is there something you can save for now which is far off in your future?
3. If you were to invest in a company by buying a share of stock, in which ones would you have interest?
4. What would it feel like to be able to help buy a car or help with college down the road?

Spending Money

An allowance gives your child the chance to have some power in decision-making. I have also found that you can avoid *some* of the struggles in the store such as, "Mom, will you buy me this?" Certainly there will always be things that I will get Peyton as her parent, but there are times when I can say, "How much money do you have?" And I don't feel so badly about *her* buying yet another toy she will play with once or twice. You can sit down together and talk about the choices your child made and how they feel about how they have used their money.

One mom says she has a conversation with her son before going into a store to set his expectations. He knows whether he is getting anything or even if they have time to look for toys that day. Genius.

Examining your own values about having and spending money is important. What messages did you receive about money when you were a child? It's amazing how our minds will store what we heard early on, and react or comply today with those early beliefs. "You must have a hole in your pocket" was one message I heard all the time. My mother had the perception I couldn't hold on to money for very long without spending it. Consequently, throughout my life I have had trouble saving money. I spend money I don't have. It goes beyond rational thinking. Until I could go back and deal with the feelings I held around that statement my parents told me, I was doomed to continue to live it out well into adulthood. It sounds wild, but it's true. Test it out yourself.

Sometimes our actions around money are formed from spending behaviors we witnessed as children. I remember my father buying a Lincoln Continental when he was in between jobs. He and my mother also went on a trip to the Bahamas at that time. I have no idea if they had the money to do these things, but I internalized that in times of transition "reward spending" is okay, instead of saving until you have regular income to pay for it.

Try This:
Money Autobiography for Parents
Writing a money autobiography may be helpful to bring out some of your deep-seated experiences. Knowing where negative patterns originated is the first step in letting them go, as well as appreciating the positive patterns.

- You can either make a timeline of your life and mark the points when significant messages and actions occurred around money;

or

- Write a narrative highlighting each message and money event.

In either case, go back to your earliest memories about money. Include your parents' attitudes and actions, as well as how you developed in your own money habits throughout your life. Do you see any similarities between your parents' attitudes and actions and your own? Are you passing any of those on to your child?

Peyton's Point of View

Spending money is very easy. You get it, you just spend it. I think you should get what you really want. My mom always says, "If you don't love it, don't get it." You could waste your money on something if you don't just love it. It's very hard to see stuff in the store that's expensive that you can't get. And the ads on TV just make me go crazy. I see them and I say, "I want it! I want it!" And I have to wait until I have more money before I can get it. It's so hard.

Questions for Reflection:
1. How have you spent your money this week?
2. How do you feel about the purchases you've made?
3. Would you do anything differently?
4. How do you handle seeing things on TV you want?
5. Have you ever gotten something and then regretted it later?
6. If you had a million dollars (for a child this just means a lot of money), how would you spend it? (The answer here might give you some insight as to what your child is thinking about on a deeper level and what values they have.)

Questions for Reflection (for parents):
1. What verbal messages were you given growing up around money?

2. What actions did you see take place around money?
3. What feelings did you have around money?
4. Are you passing those messages/feelings/actions to your children?
5. Is there anything you need to do differently?

Taking Care of What You Have

I love good, classic, quality things. Some of my clothes I have had well over a decade – and they're still in style! My home is decorated with family heirlooms and items I have picked up from my travels around the world. Each piece says something about my personality, and I treasure the meaning each holds in my heart. When something accidentally gets broken, I feel loss. I take good care of those things. I have other things about which I am less careful.

Suze Orman listed six money lessons in her recent article entitled "What Money Had Taught Me About Personal Power" in Oprah Winfrey's magazine O. One of them jumped off the page at me: "How you respect your possessions says a lot about how you respect yourself." As I look around our house, I sometimes wince and think, "What does this clutter say about what I think of myself?" Somehow I let the piles of "stuff" weigh down on me and eat away at my self-esteem. The piles of things lying around shows that I don't really value the hard earned money I spent on them – which can spiral self-esteem down even further.

If you're like this too, you can follow reverse logic. Remember how good it feels when you've gone on a cleaning spree and everything is neat and in order? You feel that you can conquer the world. You feel great about yourself and have extra energy and time to spend on other things.

Those who practice Feng Shui say you will free up energy in areas of your life if you clear the clutter. Every time I do a thorough cleaning of my home office, I find blocks which have been impeding my progress immediately start to move.

For children, it may be more complicated. They learn how to treat their things from you. So if you don't set a good example in caring for your possessions, guess what? They won't either. If children are not taught they need to put their toys away when they are finished playing, even as toddlers, they may find it difficult to put their things away as they grow older. Those habits can translate to deeper issues. As children grow, if they don't take good care of their things, they may be telling you they don't care about them. They are disrespecting their things as well as the person who bought them. It may be overt, but it is most likely an unconscious behavior. Think about it – if someone really values something, are they going to treat it poorly? No.

Granted we all have our messy moments, but there is truth here. If we don't value our things and take care of them, children will see that and do the same. And if we don't expect children to value their things, they won't. Some of this dynamic may be alleviated if children have an allowance and have the ability to use their money to buy their own things.

The lack of care of personal items can sometimes cause struggle between a parent and child. I have been guilty of saying, "If this room is not cleaned up today, I'm coming in here with a trash bag." Other parents tell me they have threatened to throw things out on the front lawn. In my case that didn't do the trick.

If you give a child clear expectations and responsibility for keeping their things in order along with the consequences if they're not done, then you're on the road to creating a more harmonious household. Children want to know their limits. They thrive on consequences (both positive and negative) and boundaries which give them a framework to live.

Here's a conversation that ends up in a lose-lose situation. Both parent and child are left with no resolution:

Parent: Your room is a mess. I told you to clean it up.

Child: Okay, okay, I'll do it today.

Parent: If you don't do it today, I'm going to come in here and throw it all out.

Child: No, Mom.

Parent: Okay, then do it.

It gets partially done but the next week the same scenario occurs. Both parent and child feel bad and the power struggle continues. The trash bag never comes out because the parent is too afraid to upset the child or doesn't want to waste the money she spent to buy new things to replace what has been thrown away!

Here's another possibility:

Parent: What's today?

Child: It's clean up my room day. (Before then, the parent and child have already gone over what "clean up my room day" entails, for example: all clothes picked up and put away, dirty clothes in the hamper, drinking glasses in the dishwasher, clutter put away, bed made, backpack cleared out.)

Parent: Okay, what did you decide the consequences are if it doesn't get done?

Child: I get my Nintendo DS taken away for five days.

Parent: Okay, just so we're clear. It's your choice. You have the power to make it happen or not.

Here the actions and consequences are clear and understood by both parent and child. The key, however, is in the follow up. That means, if what's agreed upon is not done, you follow through with the consequences. Too often parents threaten consequences they think they're "supposed" to give, but don't follow through because of guilt. Wanting your child to like you, think you're "cool," or have it better than you did, doesn't help them.

Similarly, if the agreement has been met, give positive consequences. The child has the choice over whether that happens or not. The struggle is not between the two of you, it becomes the child's own challenge ... and it works! Eventually, you don't even have to remind them that it's "clean up your room day!"

Peyton's Point of View
Taking care of your stuff lets other people know that you want more and can have more because you are responsible. When you don't trash your stuff on the floor, it shows that you love your stuff. My mom says that when you take something off, if you go ahead and put it away or put it in the dirty clothes bag, you save yourself from more work later by not putting it on the floor.

Questions for Reflection:
1. What does it feel like when your room is messy?
2. What does it feel like when the house is messy? (For example, do you want to have your friends over?)
3. Mom or Dad, complete this sentence: I feel_____ when I see you treating your things with disrespect, because it communicates_____ to me."
4. What are some ways Mom or Dad can help you take care of your things? (For example, do you need help cleaning out old things if there is too much? Do you need to set aside extra time? Buy fewer things?)
5. What are some reasonable expectations we can list for taking care of your things?
6. What are some specific consequences you can give yourself if these expectations are not met?

Saying Good-bye to Stuff

Many people have a hard time giving up the old to bring in the new. But let's face it, it must be done. I mean, you can't just keep piling up more stuff in the playroom! I always feel guilty when I sneak in a clean-out session when Peyton's not home. But when dealing with clean-out sessions together, the emotional fallout is usually very difficult.

Conversation with Peyton:

> PW: Mom! When did you throw out my stuff and what did you throw away?
>
> SW: That was when you were a lot younger, and I needed to get rid of some things so we could make room for some new things.
>
> PW: But that's not fair! I don't do that to your stuff.
>
> SW: That's true, but I get rid of things that I've grown out of on a regular basis, and when you were younger, you weren't able to do that.

We've gone through meltdowns over clothes which have to go because they are too small. I've sometimes compromised and kept a few things, hoping the next season she'll have a different response. Giving up her old bike to upgrade, though, I thought would be no problem. Her last one was three years old, and way too small for her. It wasn't quite at the point of her knees hitting the handlebars, but almost. Even the hand brakes were broken. We had purchased the bike when she asked for an upgrade a few years back. She had even raised half of the funds for it by selling some of her old toys at a tag sale.

I had heard that you could trade-up at our local bike store. So on the spur of the moment, I said, "How about we go look for a new bike today?" I had stopped by a local store earlier and had seen a bike which looked like it had her name on it – the perfect size and price and it *wasn't* pink! (Peyton hates pink.) When I brought it up, however, my idea wasn't met with the enthusiasm I expected. Nevertheless, we loaded up the old bike on the back of the car and ventured down to the store. After we handed over the bike to the nice man, suddenly it was meltdown city.

"I don't want to give my bike away," she sobbed. I held her close and didn't say a word. After a few minutes, a woman came by and said, "Poor girl, she's so sad." *Yeah, like I don't know, Lady,* I thought.

"Why don't we go upstairs and see the bike I saw earlier today?" I suggested.

"I don't like it, Mom." Maybe it was the wrong time. At any rate, we weren't leaving with that bike, and once I realized that, I let the idea go. I just sat back and tried to aid my grieving daughter.

The man gave us some time alone and whispered to me, "Thirty-five dollars" while he took the bike away upstairs. She was still sobbing. I quickly grabbed the money and took her outside, as people were definitely getting uncomfortable by now. I opened the back car door and we both climbed in. I listened as she cried, "That was my bike that I loved so much. It was such a good bike to me. We had so many memories together."

"I know you're sad," I said. Suddenly I realized that she needed me to just be there … nothing more. This wasn't about convincing her to go for the new bike. She was in the process of letting her old bike go, and it couldn't be rushed. And that was fine.

We went home, made pizza, watched a movie and went to bed. The next morning, I suggested we go to another store to look for a bike. No interest. The third time, she agreed. That afternoon, we came home with a bike – and a pink one, no less. This was such a remarkable turnaround, we talked about it at dinner a few hours later.

Conversation with Peyton:

> SW: What was it like for you to let your bike go and to get the new one?
>
> PW: It was really sad for me, because I've had it for half or a quarter of my life and I really loved it. And it was very special to me because I had it through a lot. And it's hard for me to let go of stuff.
>
> SW: Why do you think that is?
>
> PW: Because sometimes I just get so attached to it, I don't want anyone else having it. I feel like it's sort of mine. I own it. No one else can ride on it.
>
> SW: But then how do you make room for something new if you keep hanging on to the old?
>
> PW: I just try to keep as much stuff as I can, but I don't try to keep every single thing I wear. I try, but some-times I just have to let it go.
>
> SW: When you were in the middle of that did you feel that you would get to the other side of it?
>
> PW: Yes, eventually. Eventually I thought I would get through it, but it might take a day, tops.
>
> SW: And then what was it like to start thinking about a new bike today?
>
> PW: It felt like I got over it, but I still very much miss that bike, even right now. But my new bike is better….

even though it's pink doesn't mean anything!
I needed the perfect bike.

SW: What did you learn from this?

PW: I think that helped me learn to just let it go…just
like, be free, like there might be something better
than that one, one that really fits you, that you really
love. But it's always going to stay in your brain…
you'll always have it in your heart. You can imagine
it. You can pretend you still have it in your
dream world.

SW: And you make room for something new?

PW: Yeah, it's called, "One girl's garbage is another
girl's treasure!"

The bike was a biggie. We still struggle over what needs to go, and if it goes, where it goes.

Try This:
- Ask children to go through their old things to sell on e-bay or craigslist, for them to get all or part of the money.
- Pick a charity together and donate the old toys or clothes. Go there together for drop off to see the appreciation.
- Give hand-me-downs to friends with smaller children and explain she is helping out someone else.
- Ask your child's help in solving a problem, such as, "Christmas is coming. There's no room for new stuff. What do you think we should do?

Questions for Reflection:
1. Have you ever found it difficult to let go of something you've owned?
2. How did you feel about it?

3. Are you still feeling that way? If not, what turned it around for you?
4. Is there anything which you need to let go of right now? (You may both have input here.)
5. What is making it hard to let it go?
6. What can you do to help that process happen?

Our Bodies

Healthy Eating Habits

In 2002 the National Institute of Health came out with the warning "Childhood Obesity is on the Rise." With the shift toward more sedentary activities such as video gaming and computer use, and away from physical activity, children in the United States have shown an alarming trend. In her 2002 article, Carol Torgan, PhD says:

> "Obesity in kids is now epidemic in the United States. The number of children who are overweight has doubled in the last two to three decades; currently one child in five is over-weight. The increase is in both children and adolescents, and in all age, race and gender groups."

Torgan linked the amount of television watched among eight to sixteen year olds to those who were most at risk. Basically, she attributed the rise in obesity from this simple formula: too much food and too little exercise.

So just what qualifies as obese? Doctors use a measurement called the BMI or body mass index. Your pediatrician can calculate a number which is compared to a chart for all children according to weight, age and gender to determine what a healthy range is for your child.

This is serious stuff. Professionals are now seeing children at risk for all sorts of health issues they hadn't seen in previous generations. Torgan continues:

> *"Obese children now have diseases like type 2 diabetes that used to only occur in adults. And overweight kids tend to become overweight adults, continuing to put them at greater risk for heart disease, high blood pressure and stroke. But perhaps more devastating to an overweight child than the health problems is the social discrimination. Children who are teased a lot can develop low self-esteem and depression."*

Since that time, schools nationwide have gotten on board to offer a "healthy choice option" to children who buy lunch. The choices usually include whole wheat breads, fruit cups, salads, and other alternatives to the deep fried, fatty foods which had been staples in previous decades. While those healthy foods are offered on menus, administrators can't require children to eat them.

Healthy eating habits need to start at home. How many parents cook multiple dinners at night for their families just to avoid arguments and struggles at the end of the day? Let's be honest. If little Johnny or Katy will only eat pizza and chicken nuggets, that's because somewhere along the way you have allowed that to be the choice. I understand the argument, "But he won't eat it if I make it." That may be true, but if you are the parent and you say, "This is what we're having for dinner tonight," at some point, your child is going to be hungry and will eat. I realize that may sound harsh, but when you think about it, what are we really protecting them from? Healthy food? Isn't the issue more that we don't want the struggle because we don't have the energy to see it through?

Granted, I remember sitting at the dinner table staring at a plate of liver and onions long after everyone else had finished their meals and gone on to other activities. I was told to sit there until it I had eaten everything. Anyone remember the clean plate club? I knew if that stuff had gone in my mouth, I would have thrown it right back up. So, certainly making your meal choices reasonable and attractive is important.

One concept which has been very successful for getting children, especially younger ones, interested in eating more fruits and vegetables is the idea of "eating a rainbow." (See page 123). That is, eating foods of different colors to give you the full spectrum of vitamins and minerals you need.

Try This:
Here are some ideas to help if your child is overweight or struggles with food issues:
- Be supportive. Know that they are most likely already facing some teasing at school.
- Keep communication lines open with them. Explain that you want to help and support them and work on ways together to help them succeed.
- *Don't buy it*! If you don't have junk food and candy around the house, they won't eat it. And neither will you. In our house, we only have soda and juices on rare occasions. I don't buy it. Peyton has grown up loving the taste of water.
- Instead buy healthy snacks, such as popcorn (without butter), low sugar ice pops, fruit, yogurt, raisins, nuts, etc.
- Make sure you tell child care providers your desires and decisions about snacks.

- Eat meals together at the dinner table, and not in front of the TV, computer or video game console where eating can become a mindless activity.
- Have children help make dinner and make it a fun time together.
- Have a "try something new" night each week, where you explore new foods. You both might be surprised that they like more than they think!
- Cut back on pre-prepared and frozen foods which can be packed with sodium causing water retention, stress, and high blood pressure.
- Use a good multi-vitamin (we use Vemma-Next which is an excellent, doctor-recommended liquid multi-vitamin and has omega-3 minerals and an extra dose of vitamin D. It even tastes good! For more information, see resource page for details.)
- Don't use food as a reward or as a punishment. Doing so will skew your child's relationship with food during the challenging adolescent years and could possibly lead to eating disorders down the road.

Eating a Rainbow

Red fruits and vegetables may:
- Improve memory
- Maintain heart and urinary tract health
- Lower the risk of some cancers

Where can I find it? Red apples, beets, cranberries, cherries, red grapes, pomegranates, raspberries, strawberries, watermelon, pink or red grapefruit, tomatoes, radishes, radicchio, red peppers and red onions.

Blue/purple fruits and vegetables may:
- Fight aging
- Improve memory
- Reduce risk of some cancers
- Improve urinary tract health

Where can I find it? Raisins, blackberries, blueberries, plums, purple grapes, eggplant and purple cabbage, figs.

White/Brown fruits and vegetables may:
- Reduce cancer risks
- Lower cholesterol levels
- Improve heart health

Where can I find it? Bananas, white nectarines, white corn, jicama, white peaches, garlic, cauliflower, mushrooms, onions and potatoes, lentils, garlic, lentils and turnips.

Green fruits and vegetables may:
- Full of antioxidants
- Reduce the risk of some cancers
- Help maintain good eye health
- Help build strong bones and teeth

Where can I find it? Green apples, green grapes, kiwi fruit, honeydew, avocado, broccoli, spinach, zucchini, lettuce, celery and asparagus, green beans, and okra.

Yellow/orange fruits and vegetables may:
- Improve heart health
- Reduce the risk of some cancers
- Strengthen immune system

Where can I find it? Yellow apples, apricots, cantaloupe, oranges, peaches, nectarines, mangoes, grapefruit, pineapple, yellow peppers, pumpkin, corn, yellow tomatoes, lemons and sweet potatoes/yams, squash.

Mix them up. Make a game of it and see how many colors you can eat each day!

Peyton's Point of View

It's not good to always have fast food. I have pizza or french fries only once a week. I like chips, but I only have a small amount. It's not good to eat a whole lot of them. It's good to eat healthy food. If you don't, you could get fat. I have a hard time eating vegetables, but I do have a few favorites. I eat celery, broccoli and cauliflower. I also have a daily vitamin drink.

Now, candy. I love candy. Sometimes I sneak it. But I get hyper. Sometimes after I eat candy, I'll ask my mom for an apple, to be good!

Questions for Reflection:
1. What's your favorite/least favorite food?
2. What foods do you like of each color?
3. Is it hard for you to have healthy eating habits? Why or why not?
4. Is it easy or hard to eat well at school?
5. Is it easy or hard to eat well at home?
6. Do you think our family eats healthy or unhealthy? How?
7. How can we encourage each other as a family to eat better?

Bedtime

Children need sleep. Children may say they don't, but they do. It is the parent's job to set the boundary around the appropriate bed time. My mother always told me children need ten to eleven hours of sleep a night, and that's what we got. No questions asked.

In many households bedtime is an area of struggle and conflict. The television stays on, the homework gets delayed until later, the child begs for one more round of video games or says, "I'm not tired." In our house the delay tactics start right when I am ready to grab some time for myself. By that time of night, I have no more energy to be playful or clever. I find, however, if I give Peyton just one more big hug and assure her I am here for her, she goes right to sleep.

While your child may put up some fuss, a regular, reasonable bedtime is appropriate so she can function well the next day. Some parents allow their child to read in bed, if she isn't sleepy. At least she is resting. Sometimes children can't sleep because the TV is on or music is blaring or other people in the household are being too noisy. The best way to see if your child is getting enough sleep is to see how hard it is to get her up the next morning. It's as simple as that. If she is dragging, she needs to go to bed earlier. You can also watch her school performance and temperament as other clues.

Peyton's Point of View
My doctor says I should get nine to eleven hours of sleep a night. It's horrible when I stay up late because I'm always tired the next day. In the morning I'm like, "Ughhhhhhh. This is not fun. I want to sleep." If I go to bed at 8:30 or so, I wake up in the morning and go to school all energetic.

Questions for Reflection:
1. How would you describe the amount of sleep you get? Is it enough, too little, just right?
2. Are both parents and children in agreement on the household bedtimes?
3. Do you usually feel rested in the morning?
4. How easy is it for you to get up in the morning?
5. Do you have any bedtime rituals? What are they?
6. What activities do you do right before bedtime? (TV, video games, reading?)
7. Do you feel that anything needs to change around your sleeping habits?

Exercise: Move a Muscle, Change a Thought

A healthy exercise regimen for children goes hand in hand with a healthy diet. I love the slogan, "Move a muscle, and change a thought." It's true! Exercise does wonders not only for keeping your body strong and healthy but also your mind. Exercise makes people of all ages feel better. During periods of longer, strenuous movement, our bodies release endorphins which give us a natural feeling of "well-being." Our anxiety decreases and so does stress. That all translates to better self-esteem and body image. So what do you say? Let's get out there and move!

Schools are trying to do what they can to help. School districts across the country have increased the amount of physical education during school hours so kids can be more active. But some teachers say that while there has been an increase in gym activity, there has been a lowering of the demands and expectations upon the children when they get there. One teacher says she has actually received notes from a parent who complained that her child was made to run at school. She says while parents encourage their children to be active, they don't want them to be pushed to their limits because of fear that their self-esteem might be affected. Oh my goodness.

Try This:
Ideas to get your kids moving:
- Model healthy eating and exercise habits yourself. (If they see you doing pushups, and not eating the pint of ice cream that is calling your name, they may want to imitate you!)
- Plan family activities on a regular basis which involve exercise: hiking, riding bikes, walks in the neighborhood, swimming.
- Try walking places versus driving the car, when you can. It also helps the environment!

- Do activities together which support your child's self-esteem, giving them choice and power in what you do.
- Make exercising fun! If you dread it, so will they!

Peyton's Point of View
You've got to exercise! If you want to be energetic, you've got to do it. For me, if I don't exercise, I'm just going to be sitting around lazy on the couch watching TV. It helps to have my dog Max to run around with. I also like to jump on the trampoline, or play basketball or tennis.

Questions for Reflection:
1. What do you like to do for exercise?
2. Do other people in your family exercise? Do you do activities together?
3. Do you feel your body is healthy? If not, why not?
4. What things could you do be a healthier you?
5. What kind of support do you get from your family around exercise?
6. Does anything need to change?

Loving Your Body

In a girl's pre-teen life, these are the years when changes start happening in her body (see "Puberty" on page 130 for more). As girls begin to notice these changes, many start spending more time in front of the mirror. The time that it takes them to get ready to go out also takes longer. There may be multiple clothes changes before one is decided upon! It's all part of growing up in this society.

Boys of this age are noticing their bodies too, but it's a whole other deal. They may be busy with sports and building their strength. One friend, however, has a son who beginning in the second grade decided to institute a "dress up day" every Friday. While others were dressing very casually for school, he would put on a bow tie, wear loafers and nice slacks. Now that's a boy who feels good about himself! Bravo!

As girls' bodies change, it can be brutal on them emotionally. When I was in middle school two boys called me "flatsy-patsy" on a regular basis. I was devastated. Yes, I was a bit late in developing. "Who cares what other people say," Peyton responded when I told her about my experience. We talked together about whether I would share that experience in this book. She was worried that people would make fun of me again. I told her that I like what my body looks like. I added that maybe by talking about that experience so long ago, it would help someone else be able to talk about how they feel when someone talks about their body.

> SW: Are you ready to have breasts?
>
> PW: I guess so.
>
> SW: What if you get teeny ones?
>
> PW: Who cares, it's not my fault! (matter-of-factly)
>
> SW: *Exactly!*

I was a late bloomer, but these days are different. Girls are developing much earlier in life and getting noticed by boys much earlier too. They don't necessarily having the emotional maturity to always know how to handle that attention.

One mother said she hugged her third grader the other day and jokingly said, "Wow, you're breasts are getting so huge!" Her thought was that she would take an opportunity to openly talk about body image and keep it light. "Oh my gosh, I guess I'll have to start wearing a thong now!" her daughter snapped back. Whoa, baby!

I'm still fine with the fact that my daughter is chasing boys around the playground for now. The other stuff will come soon enough and my hope is that she will still feel that it really doesn't matter what other people think, as long as *she* loves *her* body!

Children often take their cues about body image from their parents. One mom with twin seven-year-old sons laughed when telling me this story. The boys still occasionally take showers with their father when they're running short on time. One day, she said her son looked at his father's private parts and said, "Dad, your penis is dead!" To which he replied, "You just wait – someday yours will be too!"

Loving your body goes well beyond loving your genitalia. How does your child love and take care of his body overall? Cleanliness, proper eating and nutrition, taking care of hair and teeth are all indicators that he feels good about himself.

Peyton's Point of View
If you feel that any of your features are too big or too small, that means that you're just not loving yourself. If you don't love yourself, you might not be happy, and that's not good. Like, just because you may have a bigger nose than everybody else, doesn't mean you're different. It just means you've got a big nose. You should always love yourself because no matter what, you will always be yourself.

Questions for Reflection:
1. Do you like your body?
2. What parts do you like best?
3. If you could change anything about your body would you do it and what would it be?

Questions for Reflection (parent to child):
1. Do you think I like *my* body?
2. How can you tell if I like my body or not?
3. What do I do that shows you how I feel about my body?
4. Do you have any concerns about how your body works?
5. Does everything feel okay inside your body?
6. Do you have any pains that we need to talk about?
7. Is there anything we need to talk to your doctor about that is concerning to you?

8. Do you have any questions for me about my health and my body?

Puberty

Just after Peyton turned nine, we read Frances O'Roark Dowell's The Secret Language of Girls together and the word "puberty" came up. "Do you know what that word means?" I asked. "No," she replied. Okay, I thought to myself, how much of 'the talk' do I do right now, and how much do I save for later when it's more age appropriate? So I launched in with some trepidation, although I never let on for a minute.

SW: Puberty is a really cool time. It's the time when you move from being a little girl to a young woman. People from all over the world celebrate it in different ways.

PW: What happens?

SW: Well, your body starts changing. Your breasts start forming and you start growing hair under your arms and around your vulva. Your body is beginning the long process of getting ready for the day when you are ready to have babies. You won't have babies for a long time (was that slick or what?), but when you get to puberty, every month your body starts a cycle of letting go of what it doesn't need. You'll see it in the form of blood, but it doesn't hurt. Different people start that process called menstruation at different ages. I was really late when I started puberty.

PW: That's why they called you flatsy-patsy (giggling).

SW: Right (thank you for reminding me, I thought!) My

breasts were small for a very long time and then
they started to grow.

At that point, I thought it would be good to add a little bit about
boys since she was still listening intently.

SW: And boys change too. They start to grow hair on
their faces and under their armpits and down by
their penis. (That got a giggle.) Their voices change
too. They get lower and they begin to sound more
like young men. During puberty, both boys and girls
have changes in their hormones which make them
feel all sorts of feelings.

By that time, I could start to see her mind was off in another place.

SW: Do you want to know any more right now?

PW: No.

SW: Okay, just let me know when you do. I want to be
available to talk to you anytime and answer any
questions. I'll make sure we talk well before you
start your period – that's another way to talk about
menstruating – so you'll know what to do. The whole
thing is really cool, Peyt.

She shook her head and looked as though she was satisfied with
what she had just heard. Looks like we got through round #1
just fine.

Puberty is a time of transitioning into adulthood. The body is
getting ready for reproduction. Given that girls generally start
puberty earlier than boys, more change may be coming sooner. In
recent years, girls are beginning to hit this stage of life between eight
and thirteen; boys range between thirteen and fourteen although
some may begin as early as nine. But each person is different and
your child's body will start this process when they are ready.

Here's what happens during puberty:

Boys:
Ears, hands and feet grow larger
Grow taller and gain bulk
Shoulders broaden and muscles get stronger
Penis and testicles increase in size
Temporary increase in breast size
Testosterone is produced as well as sperm
Voice deepens
Hair growth on face, under arms and in pubic area
Wet dreams during the night (ejaculation) and erections upon
awakening (this is normal and is caused from semen being re-
leased through the penis)

Girls:
Grow taller
Develop body contours; wider hips and smaller waist
Develop breasts (an early sign; for some girls this may be by age
nine)
Possibly have oily hair and skin; pimples may develop
Develop body odor due to increased sweating
Begin growing hair on underarms, legs and in the pubic area
Have an increase in body fat
Have vaginal discharge and lubrication
Start menstruating (age varies)
Along with menstruation, may be cramping from hormone pro-
duction, and mood swings, also known as PMS

The process for boys may take up to four years for all changes to
take place. Changes in girls' bodies may come closer together.

Many of us grew up in the age when parents were embarrassed
to talk about anything having to do with the body or bodily

functions. My mother grew up in a time when very little was explained to her at home about sexuality. Because she knew so little herself, she didn't know what she wasn't telling me.

I didn't start menstruating until I was sixteen, but when I was fifteen, I found the sanitary pad box and pamphlet sitting next to my pillow. I did try inserting a tampon before I was anywhere near starting to menstruate, just so I would be ready and would not be caught off guard. It was all so mysterious. Because we didn't talk openly about it, it took me a long time before I really felt good about most of the natural processes my body would go through as a young woman.

But times are changing. I was a little more than surprised when Peyton and I went shopping at one of her favorite clothes stores one day. At the cash register the clerk gave both of us a "free gift." Mine was a plain blue box with this message on it: "Hey Mom, Our trusted partners Procter and Gamble, makers of *Always* and *Tampax*, have provided you with a sample kit for you to share with your daughter when appropriate...."

Peyton's "gift" was a cute pink bag filled with a panty liner and wipe, a box of three tampons, a booklet entitled, "Talking with Your Daughter about Puberty" (for me) and another for her, "Uniquely Being a Girl" which has everything from a full glossary of terms, to a complete explanation and pictorial guide of the menstrual cycle, explanations of the need for hygiene, and bra-fitting information. Wow.

I was glad I looked through the information when we got home because some of the information was beyond the level we had talked about together.

SW: Are you ready to talk more about menstruation yet?

PW: No.

SW: Okay. Just checking. These booklets are good, and
    when you're ready we can talk about them, but in the
    meantime, I'll put them away. It says you can expect
    to start your period a few years after your breasts
    begin to develop. So, you let me know.

PW: Okay, Mom.

I safely tucked the boxes away, knowing they would be there when she's ready.

A friend of mine, Tom Mahoney, is a sex educator for a town in Connecticut. He is employed by the town to go into the schools and talk about sexuality. With older kids, he also talks about sexually transmitted diseases. He suggests that using the right words for body parts beginning at birth is important to set the course for future open and honest conversations as children grow up. That's the goal, right? Don't we want our children to be able to come to us and talk to us when they have problems or questions?

Unfortunately, so many of us still have hang ups about our bodies which we pass on to our children without even knowing it.

So what are the "right" words to use? Penis, vulva or vagina, and breasts are not dirty words. If we react to them as if they are and refuse to use them, then the only option children have is to think that a part of them is shameful, bad or embarrassing. Why else would we avoid calling something by its name? What is the fear behind not doing so? Do you think your child will run around the school and talk about penises or vaginas all day long? If you make a big deal out of it, and make them think it's a taboo topic, they will!

The curriculum in most public school systems, at least in the northeast, starts introducing the proper terminology for body parts in fifth grade. Classes are separated by gender. But we all know by that age, there have already been numerous casual conversations among students on the ball field, in the lunch room, at lockers and in the bathrooms.

Sexuality, which contrary to popular opinion does not mean intercourse, is simply what it means to be male or female and how one expresses it. Sexuality is a gift and it is good. Too many parents leave the education of this sacred area of life to educators in the school system, or by default to friends or eventual lovers. They miss out on discussing with their children a major part of human life. If the conversations are left to friends, it is quite possible that they may get inaccurate information.

Age-appropriate conversations about sexuality need to happen throughout childhood and into the teen years. As a framework is set at each stage, you can update the information as your child gets older. My friend Tom suggests, "Ask open-ended questions to get them to say what they heard, saw and felt about certain things."

Peyton's Point of View
To me, puberty just means you're growing older, you're going through a new phase. It doesn't seem strange at this point, it just seems like a normal thing to me. I just know in a couple of years I'm going to change. I have no idea how other kids feel about this because I don't go around and ask them "Are you excited about puberty?!" (laugh)

Questions for Reflection: (for parents)
1. In your culture, what does it mean to be a woman or a man, a girl or a boy?
2. Do you have the same expectations for your child today?
3. What other influences are present, such as religious teachings or family traditions?
4. What message did you get from your parents about what it means to be female or male? For example, some girls were told "Only boys go to college," or "The man has to take care

of the woman," or "Girls can't be smarter than boys," or "Boys have to be macho and can't show emotion," or even "The way you show someone you love them is to act mean to them."

5. Which of these messages, if any, have you passed onto your child/children? Which ones have you rebelled against?
6. How do you communicate your views of sexuality to your surrounding community?
7. Are there any expectations you want to change?
8. Are you satisfied with how you have discussed puberty and sexuality with your child thus far? If not, what else do you need to say?
9. What fears do you have?
10. When did you start puberty?
11. What was that experience like for you?
12. Are you glad to be the man or the woman that you are?
13. What words were used for various body parts like penis, scrotum, testicles, vulva, vagina, cervix, clitoris, and breasts in your family? By your peers growing up?
14. Were those words seen in a positive light or a negative light?
15. How comfortable are you saying those words with your peers? With your children?
16. What words have you used so far for body parts in your child's upbringing?
17. If you are honest with yourself, do you love your body?

Questions for Reflection: (for parents and children)
1. What does it mean to be a boy/girl? What kinds of things do boys/girls do?
2. Do you agree with all of those things and what would you add to the list?
3. How would you describe yourself? (Some terms may be tom-boy, girly-girl, boy's boy etc.)
4. How do you feel about who you are and how you present yourself to others?

5. Has anyone ever said anything to you about your body which made you feel good?
6. Has anyone ever said anything to you about your body which made you feel bad or uncomfortable?
7. What kind of changes are you experiencing in your body recently?
8. What kind of changes have you seen in your friends' bodies?
9. How do boys talk about girls' body parts, or girls talk about boys' body parts at school?
10. What questions do you have about what will happen to your body?
11. How do you feel about the changes that are ahead?
12. How can I help you as you experience these changes?
13. What other information do you need to know right now?

"Sex" vs. "The Birds and the Bees"

For many parents having "the talk" with their children is viewed as something to be dreaded. Television has given us pictures of parents stressing out as they prepare to go into another room and stumble around to find the right words to explain how intercourse happens and conception occurs. In most cases I've heard of, the conversation usually happens well after the child already knows what's coming.

Times are certainly different from when we were growing up. Children, and I mean children, are having sexual encounters earlier than many parents realize. I have heard some experts say that they know of some children in elementary school who are having or who have had oral sex. The thought is that since it's not intercourse, it is not considered to be "sex." Wow.

That idea is terrifying for most parents. The question is, how does our fear about the subject of sex color our conversation about it? Why are we uncomfortable about such a natural part of life?

When my daughter talked about the encounter she had at the lunch table in fourth grade, our conversation went something like this:

SW: Do you know what sex is?

PW: Yes. (head down yet peering up.)

SW: What do you think it is?

PW: It's when two people are laying next to each other naked.

SW: Hmmm. (I was somewhat relieved that she was wrong and wondering how much to say at this point.)

SW: Sex is when two people really love each other. The man puts his penis into the woman's vagina. But it hurts… a lot… until you get married.

UGHHHH! I was doing just fine, being the progressive mother, affirming my daughter until the end, and then my fear whipped out and overtook me out of nowhere. *I blew it.* All of a sudden her life was flashing in front of me and I saw her as a young teen having sex … and I grasped for a passing straw. I failed.

I don't want her to remember that conversation. I don't ever want her to think that intercourse hurts in any way. What I wanted to communicate, and didn't, was that intercourse, at the right time and with the right person, is wonderful and waiting for that combination to happen is a good thing.

So, just what is appropriate to say to children in the elementary school years? Again I turned to my friend Tom, who says during the elementary school years building a healthy perspective on sexuality and boundaries is key. Then as the curriculum or as children's experience dictates, parents can use conversations as teachable moments. For example, you may see something in a movie or on TV and build on the foundation from previous conversations.

In the end, he says, "We want to create a climate of trust for on-going dialogue with kids. Kids are not always going to do what we want them to do. When they do something wrong, we want them to be able to come to us and say, 'I've done something,' and trust us enough to be able to talk. Growth will come from the experience and resulting dialogue, which is a process."

Masturbation

I imagine that some of you are cringing, just reading this word. Others may be horrified that I am even bringing up the topic. Before you skip over this part, know that self-exploration through masturbation is a normal part of growing up. Many of us received extremely negative messages about masturbation when we were young. "It's nasty," or my favorite, "You'll go blind if you do it!" have been knee-jerk responses by parents who were most likely scolded by their parents when they were little for doing the same thing! How many times have you heard of a parent either slapping their son's hand away from touching his penis or shaming their daughters who have suddenly discovered their clitoris ignites extreme pleasure? (Unfortunately, many girls don't make that discovery until much later in life.)

Think about it: if we want our children to grow up to have healthy sexual lives, don't they need to know what parts of their bodies give them pleasure? Shaming the exploration translates to "your body is bad" and "pleasure is not good." Certainly there is a time and a place for everything. Encouraging them to explore their bodies in the privacy of their own room, or when they are by themselves is a good thing.

Peyton's Point of View

Ewwww…I don't want to talk about sex. It doesn't affect me. I don't think you should until you're twenty, eighty, or forty. I don't know. (See more in Boundaries: Emotional and Physical on page 141)

Questions for Reflection (for parents):

1. How comfortable are you when your child sees or hears something that is overtly sexual when they are with you?
2. How do you handle it at the time?
3. If there are older siblings around, how do you shield your younger children from topics and situations which are inappropriate for their age?
4. Has your child ever walked in on you when you and your spouse/partner were having sex? How did you handle the situation?
5. Are your children aware when you and your spouse/partner are having sex?
6. What is your feeling about masturbation?
7. What messages did you receive about masturbation when you were a child?
8. Do you encourage your male and female children to explore their bodies through their touch?
9. If so, how do you communicate that to them?
10. Is it more okay for one gender than another?
11. What boundaries, if any, have you set up with your child about where masturbation can occur?

Questions for Reflection (for parents and children):

1. What have you seen or heard about what sex is?
2. Have you ever been uncomfortable with something that you've seen or heard that you'd like to talk about with me?
3. Have you ever experienced something about your body that you would like to talk about with me?
4. Do you have any questions about your body and how it works right now?
5. Do you like your body?
6. Do you understand that as a parent I do not want you to have intercourse until you're an adult?

Boundaries: Emotional and Physical

Emotional Boundaries (for parents only)

Boundaries in relationships define where one person ends and another begins. Those lines are crucial for any relationship, especially in Western society, where individualism is a core value. As a child grows from infancy, it's a parent's responsibility to help him establish healthy boundaries. According to family expert John Bradshaw, that process cannot be hurried and must be done with care.

> "Children are egocentric because they have not had the time to develop ego boundaries. An ego boundary is an internal strength by which a person guards her inner space. Without boundaries, a person has no protection. A strong boundary is like a door with a doorknob on the inside. A weak ego boundary is like a door with a doorknob on the outside. A child's ego is like a house without any doors."

Bradshaw continues by emphasizing the crucial role parents have in the healthy development of their children:

> "Strong boundaries result from the identification with parents who themselves have strong boundaries and who teach their children by modeling."

However, some parents were raised in homes where their emotional or physical boundaries were violated. If that's the case, how can they be expected to model skills they never learned? Author and teacher Robert Hoffman explains the dilemma:

> "As children we looked to have our love needs met exclusively within the family. If our parent's behaviors in any way communicated threats to our well being, if they expressed anger, impatience, contempt, indifference, neglect, or if they abused us in any way, we felt that there was something wrong with us. As children we

*assumed that we were at fault, not them. Little by little
we came to experience the world in much the same way
as our parents."*

Hoffman developed a theory he called the "Negative Love
Syndrome" to describe how complex it becomes as we grow up
without disengaging from those earlier patterns.

*"In childhood we emulated, adopted, and internalized
(interjected) our parents' negative behaviors, moods,
and attitudes to be like them so they would accept and
love us ... Later in our adult lives we continue to com-
pulsively act out negative patterns from our childhood in
an ongoing attempt to be loved. Even though we know
that there are alternatives to our negativities, and even
though we recognize on some level that these behaviors
cannot bring us happiness, we continue to act them out."*

Hoffman developed a "Quadrinity Process" which helps participants find a way out "to release and resolve the persistent negative
feelings of being unloved and unlovable."

We all have our stuff, don't we? What baggage are you bringing into your relationship with your child? How often have you
heard yourself say something and think, "Wow, that sounded
like my mother/father?" Have you ever done something your
parents did that you promised yourself you'd never do? Seeing
the patterns and working through them is the answer. We are not
doomed to repeat the past. But to change you must be committed to the underlying emotional work. Some may simply be
able to alter their behavior through awareness. Others may
need the support of a therapist or support group to change.
For help with chronic issues, others may seek programs such as
The Hoffman Institute or The Caron Foundation, which offer
week-long programs designed for deeper work. (See reference
section for more information.)

Peyton's Point of View
You should always be able to have boundaries because maybe you want to have a secret and you need some privacy. If you don't have privacy, everyone will know everything. That's not good because sometimes you need time alone and you need to keep stuff to yourself.

Body Boundaries
In seeking good role models and caregivers for our children, we must find people who are trustworthy. Over the past decade, the media has brought to our attention story after story where adults violated the boundaries of children physically and sexually, destroying that trust. Unfortunately, children have been violated far longer than that, but only now are we hearing about those cases. The bravery of victims stepping forward is opening the eyes of the public, and breaking the code of silence to the treachery which has been occurring for centuries.

Sometimes the violators have been adults within the church and synagogue. When a religious leader crosses a sexual or physical line with a child, not only are they destroying the child's emotional and psychological development, they are severely impacting the child's spiritual development. If this violator is held up as a representative of God, and then hurts a child, how is the child to ever develop a healthy relationship with a loving God? The child as well as the whole family may never fully recover from such a breach of trust.

But what if physical or sexual boundaries are violated in the child's home? In some families there is a conspiracy of silence when abuse occurs. Members of the family may not talk about what is happening, whether it is sexual or physical violence. In some cases, the adults may not know what's going on. In others, the adults may not want to know what is happening to their children. It's almost as if they are emotionally blinded. Children become isolated and learn they can't speak up because they feel unsafe or because they feel they won't be heard or believed if they name their experience.

And it only takes one instance of abuse to create an environment where people feel like "they are walking on eggshells," waiting for the next incident to occur.

During seminary, I had the opportunity to serve as a chaplain intern in a domestic abuse shelter for women and children. There were women of every race, religion, and socio-economic background. Each had made the decision to leave their partners, some immediately and some after years of denying to themselves that the situation would change. But many women I talked to said the turning point for them was seeing the how the abuse in their homes affected their children. Many said they felt if they didn't leave, their children would be next and they were showing their children abuse is acceptable.

Fortunately, in the course of a child's life, they are around many professionals who are trained to be on the lookout for signs of abuse. Doctors, teachers, social workers, coaches, or clergy may see a behavior or hear your child say something that may be a cry for help.

The important thing is to be clear with children about what appropriate physical boundaries are, in order to create an atmosphere where you can talk openly about the topic.

According to my friend, Tom, there are life skills which can be taught throughout the elementary school years which can help prevent some incidents of boundary crossing. They are discussions about:

Information: What is appropriate and inappropriate touching and who is allowed to touch them? The answer is, "No one has permission to touch your private parts – your penis, your vulva, or your breasts – except you." And, "No one should ask you to touch their penis or vagina, no matter who they are or what they promise you."

Negotiation: The skill here is: "How do I stand up for myself and not worry about the other person?" And, "This is what is okay and this is not okay." Standing up for oneself seems to be more of an issue for girls than for boys, although some boys who are susceptible to bullying may also find themselves needing this skill. Girls are still taught to be agreeable and "nice." (Someone recently defined n-i-c-e as Nothing In Me Cares.)

When asked why one fourth-grader didn't tell her mother when asked by a boy to do something she didn't want to do, she told her mother, "I didn't want him to get into trouble. I didn't want him to not like me." Self-esteem is the issue here. Negotiation takes place when there is a give and take between two people. If one has a lower self-esteem, the exchange is most likely not going to be equally satisfying.

Refusal Skills: The ability to stand up for oneself and say "No" can be difficult if a child doesn't think they have the right to do so. They may be taught at home to "Do what adults tell you to do," or "If the pastor tells you something, do it." Refusal skills allow a child to say, "This is making me uncomfortable, so stop *now*." Or "I don't like this," "Don't do that to me," or "I don't want to do that."

For a child to be able to say "No" to something, they need to have been told what is "not okay." Children need to be given permission by a respected adult to ignore what another adult or any other person tells them to do when it does not feel right to the child. This ability to refuse allows them to validate their inner voice of truth and experience.

When Peyton was in kindergarten, I was glad when the school brought in local police to talk to the children, who reinforced the ability to say "No" when something felt wrong. Think about it: here is an authority figure telling a child it is okay to tell an adult "No" if they are asking the child to do the wrong thing. Powerful.

Self -Esteem: The United States Department of Health and Human Services says low self-esteem can be triggered by being treated poorly by someone else recently or in the past. We may also continue to carry judgments about ourselves. While some level of low self-esteem may be normal at times for adults, if it becomes chronic it can keep you from doing what you're meant to do here on this earth. Your goals and dreams may be affected. Low self-esteem can keep you in relationships which are not good for you. It can keep you depressed. If a child does not have a healthy sense of self-esteem, he or she is going to have a difficult time believing they are worthy of saying "No" to someone who is asking them to do something they don't want to do. They may be more willing to go along with the requests of others because they may feel their opinion is not as important as the person who is asking.

When an adult advocates for a child who has experienced a boundary violation, he can begin to turn around the child's self-doubt. The child can begin to think he is worthy of his own experiences, desires, and opinions.

The incident with the young boy at my church proved to me that it's always important to talk openly about what's okay and what's not okay in terms of touching, and to keep lines of communication open. That way if something inappropriate does happen, your child feels he can talk to you immediately.

From very early on I told my daughter that no one was to touch her private parts, and I still check in with her to make sure she knows her body is her body and no one else's. That message has been reiterated both at school and during doctor's visits over the years.
A friend with sons handles it similarly. She repeatedly tells them

this message: "You don't let others touch your privates. *You* can touch your privates when you are alone."

Peyton's Point of View

It's important to know that only you can touch or look at your own body…not other people. It's not supposed to happen, because it's only yours. If someone does touch you, you need to tell someone, and say "Stop. No. I don't want you to."

How I say NO to other kids:

For girls: If you have someone come up to you and ask you to do something you don't want them to do, like hugging or whatever, just stand up for yourself and say, "No." If you don't want it, you don't have to. It's not like the rule. Just 'cause they're asking doesn't mean that you have to say, "Sure." And if they peer pressure you, you can say, "Stop. No, I don't want to." Stand up for yourself – be a girl.

For boys: If a girl is doing something you don't like, same thing. You say, "No. Stop chasing me. Don't make me get body guards!" Girls can get a little crazy, sometimes.

Questions for Reflection (for parents):
1. How does this adult know my child?
2. How did they meet?
3. Do I feel good about every interaction they are having?
4. Are there any red flags I see, or is my gut telling me something is not right here?
5. How does the adult relate to me (the parent) when I am around?
6. How does my child relate to me in front of the other adult?
7. How does the adult relate to other children?
8. Are there other adults around when this person is with my child?
9. Are they spending one-on-one time together?
10. Have you noticed any difference in your child's behavior since they have known this person?

11. How do you provide a safe emotional environment for your child?
12. What do you do that invades the emotional boundaries of your child?
13. How are you like your parents/unlike your parents in your relationship with your child?
14. Who are the people in your life who are able to tell you the truth about your behavior with your children? Do you listen to them?
15. If you need help, and want to grow, do you know where to get help in your area? (see Resource section at the end of the book)

Questions for the parent and child to discuss if there is any question or concern:
1. What would you do if someone made you uncomfortable?
2. How do you like your teacher, coach, minister, etc.?
3. What kinds of things do you talk about?
4. What kinds of things do you do together?
5. What do the other children think of him/her?
6. Does this person make you feel uncomfortable in any way?
7. Does this person touch you at all?
8. Has this person ever asked you to do something which makes you uncomfortable?
9. Do you feel safe with them?
10. Is there anything you want/need to tell me?

Burps, Farts and Barf

Farts
Did you know that adult men and women fart an average of fourteen times per day? That's what a mentor of mine told me, and I believe him! So why do we have such a hard time talking about this normal bodily function? Most normal elementary school-

aged children talk about their bodily functions all the time. And if they're letting them loose, kids try their darndest to make similar sounds of farts with their mouths and with their armpits…always laughing. If you're the parent who has to listen to it, it can get old really quickly, especially if you grew up like I did.

We didn't talk about burping and farting at all! In fact, my very proper father actually called it "expelling gas!" Who in the world calls it *that*? He even punished me and sent to my room as a four-year-old when I accidentally let one loose at the dinner table, much to my mother's horror! So you can imagine, it took me a long time to be comfortable with my own bodily functions.

One day, Peyton and I were watching Nickelodeon and saw a whole segment devoted to this very topic. The narrator explained all of the different kinds of farts that exist and why people's bodies make gas … like it's a normal part of digestion! We laughed hysterically and ever since my reaction has never been the same. While still having good manners, I was able to let go of my awkwardness and let her know that I am human and can be approachable. One thing that is a carryover from my upbringing is that we always say, "Excuse me!" if one happens to slip out when we're around each other.

The body sometimes releases gas through the digestive process out of the mouth, and we've made that funny too! Burps can be loud, and smelly depending on the food item and the person. The issue comes when people who need to burp are not sensitive to others around them. No one really wants to hear another's burp. The key here is to cover your mouth and excuse yourself, should one slip out.

Did you know there are certain foods which can actually cause gas? High fiber foods such as beans, broccoli, apples are just some, as well as milk and milk products, especially if you are lactose intolerant. And carbonated drinks also cause gas. All of that fizz has to go somewhere!

Excess gas can cause stomach aches, bloating, and other discomforts, including embarrassment from the sounds and smells. Knowing and adjusting your eating habits can help to reduce any discomfort you may have.

Bathroom

There is a battle in our county: to flush or not to flush! Some parents try to conserve water. They go by the adage, "If it's yellow, let it mellow—if it's brown, flush it down!" Other parents feel not only is it good manners to flush, but it can also be a health concern! Several moms say they will actually call their children into the room every time they see a "present" left in the toilet.

Here's the conversation one mom had:

>Mom: Come here!
>
>Child: What is it?
>
>Mom: Someone left me a present.
>
>Child: I didn't do it.
>
>Mom: Go in and see whose name is on it.
>
>Child: Oh…I guess it's mine!
>
>Mom: Flush.

Ugh. Some habits are hard to break, but necessary!

And did you ever think as you flush that you could be creating a whole other problem? "If you flush the toilet without closing the lid, billions of small germy drops of bacteria are released into the air from the toilet."

Okay, are you grossed out enough yet? There's more!

Barf

I've never understood the draw of vomit. There is nothing glamorous about seeing someone's meal after they have partially digested it. Nevertheless, the pure gross factor requires this topic to have its own section.

Did you know there are websites actually dedicated to vomit? That's right. People from all over the world have chimed in with their favorite terms. Here are a few you may have heard: throw up, puke, chuck up, retch, be sick to your stomach. How about these? Blow grits, belches with speed bumps, all things re-considered, a belch too far, cash out the ATM, lose your cookies, ralph, spill your cookies, yak, oww (Cantonese for vomit), a chunder from down under (from New Zealand). For more, you can check out: www.geocities.com/mbordt/chunder2.htm.

Peyton's Point of View

(Laughing for a minute or two) They're (burps and farts) natural. My mom does them all the time. (Laughing) They're just a thing in life. When it happens you laugh. It's no big deal but it's a little stinky sometimes! (More laughing.)

Questions for Reflection:
1. Why do you think so many people laugh about these bodily functions?
2. What is the attitude in your house around burping, farting, barfing and bathroom humor?
3. When is it appropriate and when is it inappropriate?
4. Do you have different guidelines when you are at home vs. out in public? What are they?
5. What guidelines do other people you know have about these bodily functions?
6. What would it be like if you let a burp or a fart loose out with other people?
7. Have you ever thrown up in front of others? What was it like?

5

In the Community

It Takes A Village...

We've all heard the phrase, "It takes a village to raise a child."
Secretary of State Hillary Clinton even used the phrase as the
title of her book which discussed the role individuals outside the
family have on children's lives in the United States.

The origin of the phrase comes from several African cultures,
where there is deep respect and value for the place of community
in one's life. Elders remain within the community, tribal customs
are adhered to, and cultural values are followed closely. Truly, the
village as a whole has a role in raising its children.

Many in our North American culture have learned to embrace
more of an individualistic lifestyle. We are transient. Our work
takes us to other regions of the country and many no longer stay

as close to extended family members as in previous generations. For some, friends become like family. But for others, the isolation puts a strain on the family unit. In many families where there are two parents present, both have to work to merely make ends meet. Children are left to be cared for by daycare professionals, babysitters, or neighbors. Some are lucky to have family members as caregivers.

As a single mom, I have struggled with the questions of how to get quality childcare while juggling work hours so I can spend as much time with my daughter as possible. For me that has meant changing some priorities at work, and refusing some odd-hour freelance shifts which keep me away from home at night.

But even for families where a parent is able to be home with their child, there are still many other adults who will have a significant impact on the child's life: teachers, clergy, other parents, babysitters, neighbors, coaches, doctors, mentors, therapists, and so on. Each can offer our children certain things which parents can't – an unbiased voice, for one.

I want my daughter to learn from as many safe and responsible adults as possible. We have developed relationships with neighbors who are almost surrogate grandparents, since her grandmother lives states away. Here's what Peyton has to say about our neighbors Bern and Josephine:

"The things I like about having Bern (I call him the Bernstein) and Josephine (I call her Jo) next door are that they are always there for me, like when my mother asks them to babysit me. Whenever they go on vacation they always bring me back a present or send me a post card! They play with me, too. One day when it snowed, Jo came over and made a snowman and then a fort with me and then we made ice cones. When there's trouble I know they can always help me. I like that I can trust them in situations. I can count on them and I think they can count on me, too."

Another mother told me her son goes next door to an older neighbor's house and they tinker on cars together, something neither she nor her husband have any desire nor ability to do. One day her son came home holding some mysterious car part and proudly said, "Mom, look at the prizes Joe gave me!" That boy was not only learning about auto mechanics, but about teamwork, strategy, and how to relate to someone older. The boy and his brother help Joe snowplow and rake leaves. They ride on the tractor in the big field out back, priceless interactions that leave both boys and Joe enriched.

Religious communities also provide opportunities for community building and mentoring to occur. For almost three decades, I have had the privilege of taking high school students away for an annual work camp experience. We've traveled together internationally as well as domestically and I have watched young lives change right in front of me, as these youths have opened themselves to new experiences. The conversations which take place during these work camps can be deep and formative in a young person's life. I thank the parents of these teens for having entrusted their children's young lives into my care.

Childcare

This could be a whole book by itself. Very few households across the United States can afford to have one parent stay at home to care for the children. Fortunately, since the women's movement, there are more choices available for parents today and companies are much more open to providing working parents the option of flex-time and telecommuting from home, knowing that happy parents end up being better workers.

I understand the complexities of working moms, in particular. Perhaps mom is working to make money to run or support the household. Perhaps she has the desire to make a contribution in the larger world. She may have guilt over missing school events, and regret over missing milestones in her child's life. She may experience anxiety over another person having an influence in her child's life.

When I went through my divorce, I split my time between working at my church and as a freelance TV news reporter. My news shifts were mostly undesirable – either very early or very late. There were few times when I got a daytime shift. As soon as I separated, I told the station that I would be unable to do the early morning shift anymore. I still was working some at night, which required me to have a sitter with Peyton until 11 pm. As time went on, I had to weigh the costs of missing both the important and the everyday events in her life with the income from a day's work. I chose to cut back, but I still needed some childcare a few days a week. Even then, the juggling act and anxiety persisted. One time I was getting ready to go live on television with a news report, when my sitter called me on my cell phone and said she was stuck in traffic and would not be at the bus stop when my seven-year-old arrived. Ugh. Fortunately, a neighbor came to the rescue.

How do you choose the person who will be a regular influence in your child's life when you are at work? We've had some excellent sitters and some really bad ones. One time Peyton's father came home at 7 PM to find the sitter and our daughter (who was five at the time) hiding behind the couch throwing popcorn out into the middle of the room. The popcorn, by the way, was what Peyton had asked for and gotten for dinner! Needless to say, that sitter didn't last long.

Then there are those babysitters who are like gold – those who contribute to the life of your child and can become mentors.

Conversation with Peyton:

> SW: Who have been some of your favorite babysitters?

(She named a few.)

SW: What makes them your favorites?

PW: They have to be fun and they have to be responsible.

SW: How do you know if they are responsible?

PW: If they can tell me what to do… and I don't have to
 tell *them* what to do.

SW: It sounds like you like babysitters whom you respect?

PW: Yeah.

I have learned to listen to Peyton when she says she doesn't like a
particular sitter, because I know she will not behave as well for her.
And because she is so smart, as children are, she is able to sniff out
when she is able to wrap someone around her little pinkie during
their first encounter!

Try This:
Tips for Finding a Good Caregiver
 • Ask people you trust for referrals.
 • Check at local houses of worship and area colleges
  for suggestions.
 • Call local pre-schools for teachers who want extra work.
 • Make sure you get several references, and call them
  before hiring.

Questions for Reflection:
*(For use after a new sitter. You can also use these to check back in
after he/she has been with you for some time.)*
 1. Did you like the babysitter? Why or why not?
 2. Did you feel he/she listened to you?
 3. Did you feel safe with him/her?Did you feel if
  something went wrong, they would know how to
  handle the situation?
 4. What did you do when he/she was here?

5. What did the sitter do when he/she was here?
6. Did you feel you could get away with anything?
7. Do you want me to ask this sitter back?
8. Who are some of the adults in your life who have made a difference to you?
9. What have you appreciated about them?
10. How can we let them know they are important to you?

Questions for Reflection (for parents):
1. Do you like this person?
2. Is your child safe with this person?
3. Does this person have good boundaries with your child?
4. Is she clear with your child about what the child can and cannot do?
5. Does she follow your instructions regarding expectations and discipline?
6. Does this person have good boundaries in regard to your possessions?
7. What kinds of things will your child learn from this person? (Both positive and negative.)

Being Open to Difference

During the mid 1980's I worked in Japan for a year teaching English conversation in a small church. My teaching partner, an African-American man, and I worked in a small suburb of Tokyo; two of the few, if not the only, North Americans living there. During that year, my eyes were opened. I experienced, on a very small scale, what it is like to be treated differently just because of the color of my skin. It was an extremely important lesson for me to learn, one which so many here in this county experience every day. I made a vow at that time to continue to put myself in situations where I was around people who are different from me, no matter how uncomfortable it may seem at the time. Experiences which stretch me out of my "comfort zone" keep me learning and experiencing from new perspectives.

That philosophy is important in my parenting also. I am committed to raising Peyton with the sense that just because someone may look or live differently from us doesn't mean they're wrong or bad. Difference is good. In fact, she and I have different cultural backgrounds, and that is good. But by connecting to the heart of another, even when they look different, we expand our ability to be compassionate.

It helps to live in an area of the country where people show a rainbow of color, culture, ability, and sexual orientation, so we can talk about how difference impacts us. One of Peyton's friends has a father who is African-American and a mother who is a Caucasian Russian Jew. I asked his mother, who happens to be a social worker, how she explains difference to her son and daughter. She said, "When he's brought it up, I am honest. I don't want him to be ashamed or embarrassed. Mom is white and Dad is black and you're half and half." Interestingly one of her children has identified more with Caucasian culture and the other with African-American culture. It's all good to her.

Accepting difference in others doesn't mean you have to agree with them, only that you treat them with dignity and respect. The intolerance of others has lead to some horrific events in our world's history: the Holocaust, 9/11, slavery, acts of hatred by the KKK, and many others. Isolating ourselves in homogenous groups is not the answer.

When you think about it, we're all different in some way. Some differences are just more obvious than others. Unfortunately, if children aren't taught that differences are normal and acceptable, they can grow up to be bullies, prejudiced or self-haters. None of those options are what I want for my daughter.

I hate to admit it, but when I was in my early twenties, I was extremely intolerant of many groups of different people. I negatively judged gays and lesbians, and anyone who wasn't my brand of "Christian." I was self-righteous and insufferable. It took living in Japan for a year for me to change. I experienced a deep crisis of faith. I began to face my deep-seated fears of others who believed differently from me, as well as my rigidity. I began the long journey of letting go of the old and rebuilding something new. It was an agonizing and holy struggle but transforming and life-giving. In the process, I became more compassionate with myself and others, and which led me to commit to raising my daughter to welcome the fullness of God's diverse creation.

How do you talk with your children about people who look and act differently? Whether it's someone of a different race or culture, someone who has a physical disability, someone who lives in a big house or is homeless, your child will recognize how she is different from that person. The question is, how do you deal with it?

When Peyton was six years old, the organist from my former church and her partner decided to have a Holy Union ceremony. Gay marriage was not yet legal in Connecticut. Charlotte and Marge are dear friends and had loved Peyton since she was adopted. So when we were both invited to their ceremony, I decided this would be a great thing for Peyton to experience. I also wanted to be there to support them. Marge had been living with cancer for some time and I didn't know how much longer they would have together, and in fact, several years later, Marge died.

Whether you agree with this idea or not, one thing is for sure: after two decades together, Marge and Charlotte's love was tried and true. As we sat in the packed church sanctuary and they proclaimed their love and dedication to one another, Peyton turned to me and said, "Mom, this is just weird!"

I smiled and said, "I understand why you feel that way. This seems weird to you because you've never seen it before. But honey, they love each other and they are committed to each other and to God. This is how they want to express that love and commitment, and I want to support them."

That was enough for her right then. During the reception she had a great time, especially since she got to play with the balloon animals on the tables. And she came away having experienced something out of her comfort zone. I believe she is better for it.

Peyton's Point of View
Groups of people sometimes exclude other people. It's not nice. It can hurt their feelings. I don't get why they do it, because we're really all the same. If I'm around people who are different from me, it makes me want to be nice and make a good impression.

Questions for Reflection (for parents):
1. How were people who are different from you discussed in your house as a child?
2. Were your parents prejudiced?
3. Are you overtly or covertly prejudiced?
4. How does your child relate to others who are different?
5. Do you encourage interactions with children who are different or do you steer clear?
6. How have the two of you talked about those who are different than your child?

Questions for Reflection (for parents and children):
1. How do you feel about children who are of a different race than we are?
2. Think about your group of friends. Are any of them different from you in any way that stands out?
3. Have you talked about your differences?

4. Does it make any difference to them that you're different?
5. How do other children treat that child?
6. Do you know anyone who has been made fun of because they are different?
7. Do you feel different in any way?
8. What kinds of things does your school do to help people who are from different groups get along?

You're a Citizen of the World: Know Your Heritage

Western tradition often isolates us from the rest of the world. Even though this country is a "mixed salad bowl" of many different cultures, our news reports on television and newspapers often don't tell us what is going on in other parts of the world. As a parent of a child of international adoption, I want to raise my daughter with a sense that she is a citizen of the world and connected to her roots.

A few years ago, my older sister started exploring our family genealogy. She spent hours upon hours researching our family tree and ethnic roots and then gave each of her siblings a series of thick notebooks tracing back our lineage.

For one momentous birthday, she asked me if I would take a trip with her to Texas to search out my namesake, who had held land outside of Houston. We had a ball together, walking through graveyards and striking up conversations with local townspeople about our long-past relatives, who were still known in the area. I was reminded how small the world is when we went into a small town antique store and asked if they knew of a distant relative who we thought was still living – and they did! We drove a few blocks, knocked on the door, and spent the next few hours visiting and sharing memories with a woman who helped put some of the pieces of our history together.

Peyton doesn't have that luxury. She was born in Moscow, Russia and adopted at the age of one. I know only a little of her history based on the paperwork I was given by the orphanage where she spent her first year of life. But during the four weeks that I spent in Moscow, as I waited to take her home, I gained such an appreciation of her native land. Russia is extremely rich in tradition, history, art and culture. The people are warm and gracious and have lots of stories to tell.

Since we have been home in America, I have felt it is important for Peyton to learn as much about Russian culture as possible. We are fortunate to live in the New York metropolitan area where there are many people with Russian heritage. She has been able to take Russian language classes, attend Russian festivals, and even visit neighborhoods where Russian is the preferred language.

I'll never forget the time her father and I took her to Brighton Beach to celebrate the anniversary of her adoption. As soon as she got out of the car, her face lit up because she recognized the writing in Russian on the sides of the building. By that time she had been taking Russian language classes for a few years, and while she couldn't understand it all, she did recognize the letters and could pronounce the words. I could feel the pride swelling up inside her. There was a sense that she was "home" even if it was thousands of miles away from the place of her birth. A portion of herself that had been tucked away in American culture was able to be free as we heard the babushkas (grandmothers) chattering away with one another. She was able to see what her fellow country people look and sound like and how much she looked like them. It was almost as if a missing piece of the puzzle was found, if only for a few hours.

At the end of the day, Peyton was glad to travel back to our home an hour or so away. She wasn't able to explain what that visit meant to her. Perhaps to know that place exists, and more importantly, that a whole country exists that awaits her return, was reassuring on some level.

Some day we will go to Russia, when Peyton is ready, and when we do, she'll go there with some sense that she is part of this vast, mysterious, wonderful culture that contributes to who she is.

What is your child's cultural heritage? Whether your background is first generation from another country or many generations ago, it is important to provide opportunities for your child to know something about the roots and customs of her ancestors. Even if you don't live in or near a community that has people from your culture, you can read about the people or make a trip there someday. Religious communities often are good places to find celebrations of some cultural traditions. Music is another great way to get inside a culture.

Peyton's Point of View
Peyton wants to keep her thoughts private on this topic.

Questions for Reflection:
1. What are your cultural roots? Make a family tree to show what countries family members came from.
2. What were some of the challenges your ancestors faced as they grew up?
3. What are some of their achievements or contributions they made to society?
4. What aspects/customs of your cultural background do you continue today?
5. Why is it important that you do those things?
6. Are there any traditions that you and your family can begin now to honor your ancestors?
7. Do you have any artifacts from your ancestors in your house?
8. What do they mean to you?

Manners

When I was growing up, "Miss Manners" had a regular column in the local newspaper. There was a little picture of her above her advice. She was a prim and proper looking lady and I felt that I might look like her if I did what she said. She fielded questions from readers about what was and was not appropriate action for any given situation. I lived in a household where my parents expected good manners on a daily basis and Emily Post's rules of etiquette were referred to on more than one occasion. I appreciate their guidance, though, because my parents wanted to make sure that I could handle any given situation that came my way.

Simply put, manners are the ways we interact with others, how we talk to them, treat them, interact with them. Unfortunately in our world today, many children are not taught manners. Maybe because their parents never learned themselves, maybe the parents don't think manners are important, or they think manners make someone look stiff and artificial. Maybe certain manners don't fit into a particular cultural background. I don't know.

However, teaching your child "good manners" is important. Good manners are estimable acts. They teach respect for others and for yourself. When you treat others with respect and you treat yourself with respect, you can't help but build your self-esteem. Everyone wins!

Peyton's Point of View

It's not that table manners are hard, it's just sometimes they are annoying. You always have to sit up straight, and chew with your mouth closed, don't eat with your fingers. Sometimes you just want to lay low and forget about them. But you need to do them, because you don't want to embarrass yourself and have people talking behind your back.

A. THANK YOUS (WRITTEN AND VERBAL)

Saying "thank you" after receiving a compliment or when someone does something nice for you is acknowledging a gift they have given to you. Just think about it. Someone has taken the time to let you know how special you are either through words or action. The least we can do is respond with a "thank you!"

Try This:
Just practice how it feels to *not* say thank you. Somebody deliberately does or says something nice to another person and the other person doesn't say anything. How does that feel?

We want to be acknowledged for the things we do. Thank yous go a long way to creating good will with other people. Thank yous show courtesy when interacting with the world around you. By telling someone "thank you" we take part in creating a better world!

Writing a "thank you" can sometimes be even more powerful than a verbal one. Ever since I was a young girl, my mother and father expected me to write thank you notes whenever I got a gift. In fact, notes became so expected in my extended family that I would get a call from a relative within two weeks after the gift had arrived if they had not received a note from me. They would politely ask, "Did you receive my gift?" I eventually learned that it was easier to write the note sooner than later.

Even though it is like pulling teeth sometimes to get Peyton to write a note after a birthday or Christmas has passed, I am always amazed at the creativity that comes out when I read what she has written. It also helps her to keep in touch with relatives who live far away. And I'm not talking about emailing to say "thank you." I mean taking out a note card or piece of stationery and writing a note that has to be mailed through the postal service. Writing letters is a lost art these days. The note doesn't have to be long or fancy. As the old saying goes, "It's the thought that counts."

So when do you write a thank you note?
- After receiving a gift.
- After someone does something nice for you.
- After an important meeting when you want to be remembered. (One friend wanted to send her daughter to a new school and after meeting with the new principal, she sent a thank you note while she awaited their decision. You can bet that little extra effort made an impact on the principal.)

Peyton's Point of View
Writing thank you notes is probably the hardest of the manners for me. First you have to remember what you got, then you have to write down what you liked about it. But it's important to do it because it lets people know you like what they got you and it makes them feel good.

Questions for Reflection:
1. How do you feel when someone thanks you for something you've done or for something you've given them?
2. Have you ever not been thanked for something when you think you should have been? What did that feel like?
3. How about writing a thank you note to someone who will be totally surprised by it. How does it feel to do that?

B. TELEPHONE ETIQUETTE:

The topic of telephone etiquette came up after we read a book about a girl who called someone and didn't identify herself. She expected the person on the other end of the telephone to know who she was. Since this also happens to be one of my pet peeves, we took time to discuss it. It's embarrassing for me to have to put out so much effort on the other end of the line, thinking to myself, "Okay, just keep on talking and maybe I'll figure out who this is."

So how do you answer a telephone?
"Hello."
The other person says,
"Hello, this is Peyton, may I please speak with Sarah?"
"Just a moment, please."

Or, if Sarah happens to answer the telephone:
"Hello, this is Peyton, may I please speak with Sarah?
"This is she!"

If the person is not there, you might say:
 "I'm sorry, Peyton is not here right now, may I take a message?"

When Peyton was in the third grade, a boy called her several times and asked to speak with her. When I asked who it was, all he said was, "a friend." That response doomed him in my eyes right then. He later told her to lie to me and tell me he was really one of her girlfriends. Double doom. *Never* lie to the mother of a girl you're trying to impress. Didn't he realize he has to come through me to get to her? Obviously not. Wrong move, buddy!

One mom with an adolescent daughter told me about a boy who called her daughter. When he asked to speak with the young teen, Mom said, "Wait a minute, you've got to talk with me first. I need to know who you are and what you're about." She proceeded to talk with the sixth grade boy, who I'm sure after that conversation would never dream of treating any girl with anything but the utmost respect. When the daughter objected, Mom said, "Listen, don't ever go with a boy who won't talk to your mother. You deserve to be with a boy who can talk to your parents."

C. COMPUTER ETIQUETTE OR "NETIQUETTE":

Children begin learning how to use computers at an early age, either at home or at school. Etiquette is just as important when dealing with someone on the computer as it is in person or on the phone.

Here are some guidelines to watch for and discuss together:
- Be kind and careful how you say things. Words written in email or in other text doesn't have a voice attached, so others don't know how it's meant.
- DO NOT USE ALL CAPS – people will think you're yelling at them.
- Return emails promptly.
- Don't give out personal information to strangers. To friends, always put your name on it, rather than let people guess who it is.
- Don't use bad or inappropriate language. Not only does it reflect badly on you, it is hurtful to other people.
- Don't break the law. Just because you're on a computer, doesn't mean you can do whatever you like. There are laws in cyberspace just like there are in real life.
- Do not ever speak badly about other people or threaten other people online. You can get into big trouble and you never know who will ultimately read it.
- Assume whatever you write or whatever pictures you post will be out in cyberspace forever! Years down the road when schools and potential employers look on your Facebook page, do you want them seeing what you are posting today? That goes for kids as well as parents.
- Don't react immediately. Pause. If someone writes you an email that is mean or hurtful, take a break and don't shoot back at them. See if you feel the same way another day.

As children begin to use email, parents need to be clear about the limits and boundaries of their Internet usage. So many of us fear our children will think we are intruding into their lives if we ask questions or look at the web sites they've been using. Look and listen, but do it with great respect and openness and talk about why you are doing it. A parent's motive should always be clear: the safety and health of your child.

Questions for Reflection:
1. When can your child use the computer at your home? (Days of the week and time of day.)
2. What sites are appropriate for your child to browse?
3. Do any of the sites require parental consent or have minimum age requirements?
4. What information does your child need to provide? (Never use their real names in a children's online name or profile)
5. Do you use parental controls? If so, which websites have you agreed upon as appropriate?
6. What boundaries have you set up regarding parental review of websites and email?
7. What consequences are in place if agreements are not kept?

D. GREETING SOMEONE IN PERSON:

How you greet someone in person says a lot about who you are and how you feel about yourself, no matter what your age. When you greet someone, you are, in effect, presenting yourself to the world. If your head is droopy and you're looking down, you meet the world that way. If you stand up straight and present yourself with confidence, you meet the world in a better way.

Once I was a witness to a woman helping her young son learn this lesson. The woman was married to a celebrity. She introduced the boy, who was no more than five years old, to another adult. She gently said, "Look her in the eye, shake her hand firmly and say, 'It's nice to meet you, my name is James.'" Chances are, this boy will have high-level public figures in his house as he grows up, but he learned that morning that you treat everyone the same, no matter who they are. The mother showed her son that not only is he worthy of respect, but so is the person he is meeting.

If you meet someone and you're not feeling very good about life at that moment, the phrase, "Fake it until you make it" works really well. That means even if you're not feeling welcoming at the moment, going through the motions until you do will eventually get you there. Your intention can create your reality even if you're feeling insecure.

E. TABLE MANNERS:

My parents were big on table manners. In fact, my father would interrupt any of us in the middle of a conversation to correct something that was out of line. While I wouldn't necessarily recommend that, his care and interest in how my sisters and I presented ourselves to others was communicated.

As I raise my own daughter, I loosened the reins a bit, but I have told her, "I want you to be equally comfortable eating with the Queen of England as well as a homeless person."

- The first thing you do when you sit down is put your napkin in your lap. That's where it stays until you are finished eating. Then it is tucked under the side of your plate.
- Always wait to eat your first bite until the host or whoever cooked the meal takes the first bite. When a crowd is hungry, I know this can be hard, but this action shows respect and appreciation for the time the person took to put it all together.
- Don't talk with food in your mouth. I still remember a friend turning to me at the fifth grade lunch table. She

started talking to me and her mouth was full of egg salad! Yuck! I could never eat egg salad after that. Thinking back to that scene still grosses me out!

- Chew with your mouth closed.
- Don't slurp your soup or drink. (Unless you're in Japan where it's culturally acceptable. Slurping and burping after eating shows the hostess you enjoyed the meal!) Peyton says, "I want to go to Japan!"
- Sit up straight in your chair.
- Keep your elbows off the table and the hand not in use in your lap.
- Cut bites of food which can easily be chewed and swallowed, and while you're chewing, put your utensils down.
- Use your utensils unless you're eating finger food. In some cultures in Africa and parts of the Middle East it's acceptable for people to eat with their hands.
- If you'd like some more, you can ask by saying, "May I please have some more?"
- When you are finished, and want to leave, "May I please be excused?" is a good way to ask. And don't forget to say "Thank you" to the person who put it all together!
- Always clear your plate from the table. In our house, Peyton has had the job of doing the dishes since she was eight years old. That means clearing the table, rinsing the dishes and putting them into the dishwasher. I still clean the pots and pans. This lets her know she is part of the whole dinner experience. And I try to remember to say, "Thank you!" when she's done!

F. OTHER MANNERS:

- Stay to the right when you're walking down the street, on a stairway, or riding on a bike path, just like in driving (unless you're in England, Japan, or another country where it's normal to drive on the other side.)

- Open the door for other people and hold it open until they go through.
- Give up your seat for a pregnant, elderly, or sick person.
- When asking for something, always say, "please." (Hint: there's a much greater chance you will get what you want!) And after they've given it to you, remember to say, "Thank you!"
- Look at someone when they talk to you and when you answer them.
- Don't interrupt someone when they are talking.
- Cover your mouth when you sneeze! And then say, "Excuse me!"
- If someone asks you to return a call or to respond by a certain date, do it!
- Don't take what's not yours. Plain and simple!
- Tip, if the service is good. The average tip is 15-20% for food and other services. Obviously children don't usually have this responsibility, but if they don't see you as an adult doing this, they're not going to learn it. This is another way of saying "thank you" for the service they've been given.

If you're from a culture other than the United States, or if you've visited other countries, what are some of the differences in cultural cues? I try to study as much as I can before I travel to make sure I don't offend the people who live there. For example, one custom in the southern part of the United States is for people to look at each other in the eye as they pass on the streets and smile and say "Hello!" In some countries, however, if a person makes eye contact he will be viewed as rude and forward.

Finally, no book on parenting elementary school-aged children would be complete without talking about – nose-picking! Every child does it at one time or another (adults do too, by the way.) I remember kids who were made fun of because someone saw them picking their nose and then…yuck of all yucks…the unthinkable …they ate the bugger. (Even writing it down makes me cringe!)

My sister the teacher gives the "Bugger talk" at the beginning of every year. "They'll be no nose picking and then eating it in the class…that's just gross. There's no nutritional value in them and if you pick them, they'll end up somewhere where I will touch it. Since you don't want to see me throw up, don't do it." She says they all laugh out loud at her honesty, but she reminds them, "They are funny to talk about but it's disgusting in reality! You can laugh, but you know who you are!" She makes sure to make it funny, but believe me, she's serious – my sister has always been good about being direct!

She says her behavior modification program begins with the "talk" as well as the addressing of the public health issues involved. Then after a few weeks, she'll redirect the child's attention if she sees him digging in class. If the child continues over the next few weeks, she'll nonchalantly drop a Kleenex by his desk as she walks by. Then, she says if the child is still "going for it" in class by Christmas, she'll just look at him and say, "Stop it!"

Another mother says her sons call them "bickies!" (I don't know, but just making the name cuter doesn't make it any better for me.) She said she hasn't found a way to stop it, but tries at least to call attention to this action which she finds repulsive. At first she says she tried to motion to them to cover themselves when they did it, but that didn't work. Now she says she blurts out, "Did you get a winner?" One of her sons (and maybe even her husband) will yell back, "It's an 8…Bingo!" She says with a sigh, "Maybe better luck next time."

Questions for Reflection:
1. Which manners are most important in your family?
2. How did you decide upon those?

3. What do those manners reflect to others both inside and outside your family unit?
4. Which are easiest/hardest to keep?

Taking What's Not Yours

"Mom, Johnny took my favorite video game without asking." We've all heard something similar if we have more than one child in the house. It may seem innocent but learning at an early age to respect what's mine and what's yours is important. Teaching your child sharing and negotiating skills as toddlers is the first step. If those skills aren't in place when children get to elementary school years, conflict may arise. If it becomes a regular occurrence, parents need to keep watch to make sure something deeper isn't happening.

Many children shoplift. The National Association for Shoplifting Prevention has the numbers: each year more than 13 billion dollars of goods are stolen from retailers; 27 million, or 1 in every 11 people do it; 25% of shoplifters are kids. Peter Berlin, founder of the NASP says juvenile shoplifters usually are motivated by family, school, and peer pressures. "While teens, like adults, usually know the difference between right and wrong, when their life becomes too stressful they become more vulnerable to temptation, peer pressure, and other things that can lead them to shoplift. This is especially true when they feel unworthy, angry, depressed, unattractive, or not accepted."

If you think your child may be shoplifting, keep a watchful eye and ask direct questions. If you find that he has stolen something, make him accountable. I have heard many a parent tell of accompanying her child to a store, having the child return stolen items, and apologizing to the store manager.

One video store owner says his youngest shoplifters are elementary school-aged boys. He gave an example of a boy who often traded in used video games to "trade up" for an Xbox. The owner didn't question this behavior, because he knew the boy and his family. One day, the boy's parents came to the owner with a list. "Did our son bring in…" and they listed about ten video games. The owner said he had. The parents told him the games had all been stolen from his siblings and schoolmates. They asked the store owner to ban their son from the store. The owner agreed. A year later when the boy came in to try to do business again, the owner refused the sale.

Even if you have raised your child with a strong moral compass, she may still shoplift and bury the consequences. I did it twice when I was in elementary school. One time I was with a friend in a candy store. We both slipped some candy into our pockets, and were run out of the store by the clerk. The second time I was shopping alone in a women's boutique. I saw a pair of women's earrings that I liked. I took one of them. (Oh, brother!) That time I didn't get caught and I never told anyone until adulthood when my sister and I played a "tell all your secrets" game with our mother. Why did I take it? I don't know. I liked it. I wanted it. I felt a rush. I felt shame, but I did not talk about it.

At a point in my adult life when I was making peace with myself and others, that shoplifting incident came to mind. On some level it was still eating away at me. I knew if I wanted to lead a life of integrity and be truly free, I needed to do something, even though it may have seemed insignificant at the time. I checked to see if the boutique was still in business to make some kind of restitution. It wasn't, so I made a donation for a specified amount to an organization which helps women in need.

If the research is correct, over six and a half million kids shoplift a year, and those are the ones who are caught. Chances are your child or someone your child knows will shoplift at some point in their lives. The NASP says, "55% of adult shoplifters say they started in their teens." That tells me that parents need to be aware. (For more information see www.shopliftingprevention.org.)

Peyton's Point of View
I haven't been tempted to steal. It would just be too sad for me to see someone say, "Where's my thing? Where did it go?" It would probably hurt me more than it would hurt them, because I would be feeling guilty. It would be hard to confess if I did it. If you have taken something from someone, it's good to feel guilty about it. It doesn't mean you're a bad person, it could just hurt the other person you took it from. If you have taken something, return it. Say you're sorry. Why not write them a letter?

Questions for Reflection:
1. Have any of your friends ever dared you or suggested that you steal something?
2. What would you say to him if he did?
3. Have you ever had thought to take something from a store without paying for it?
4. What did it feel like?
5. What made you take it/not take it?
6. What do you do when you are feeling angry, or depressed, or bad about yourself?
7. Do you ever want to "act out" or "get back" at someone by taking something?
8. Do you know what the consequences are if you steal something? Outline the consequences from the parent and the legal ramifications.
9. Do you know that I do not want you to steal?
10. Have you ever seen me (the parent) do anything which makes you think stealing is okay?
11. Do you feel that you could come to me if you were in trouble?
12. Is there anything we need to talk about right now?

Heroes

Everyone looks up to someone. Heroes are said to show great courage in the face of adversity. They are important because we look to them as role models of the best life has to offer. In heroes, we see character traits and values we want to emulate. We see models for success and gain hope and strength when we see how they have faced adversity in their lives. We need to see people who have reached their dreams and who have gone further than we think we can go. Witnessing such success helps raise our sights beyond our sometimes limited imaginations.

We have a marvelous example in Barack Obama, whether you like him or not. I remember seeing interview after interview on television of children and adults of color saying that when President Obama was elected, it gave them hope that they could be anything they wanted to be. That single event shattered the glass ceiling for countless people who had based their expectations of the future on the reality of the past. President Obama became a symbol of hope for thousands of people of what "could be."

Others might look to Sandra Day O'Connor, a retired Supreme Court justice who was the first female to serve in that position. Justice O'Connor was appointed by former President Ronald Reagan and forged a new way for women on the highest court of the country.

While we need to have heroes, it is equally important to tell your child that they are people – mere human beings. They may have done amazing things and faced tremendous odds, but we are all fallible, nonetheless. Throughout history many of those we have put on pedestals have fallen off due to scandals or human flaws. We do a disservice to our heroes and to ourselves to put people on pedestals. By doing so, we prevent ourselves from relating to them as people who may have done something amazing, or who may be tremendously talented, but who are still human. In addition, if we think our heroes are so far above us then we'll never think hard work and focus can attain what they did. It's important to remember you can make mistakes and still be great. It's all a matter of what you do with what you've got.

HEROS AND IDOLS

Note: There is a difference between a hero and an idol. An idol is someone you adore for exterior reasons; a hero is someone who is admired for a special achievement, strength or courage.

Try This:
Who are your child's heroes and heroines? Who are yours? You may not need to look further than the posters on your child's bedroom wall to get an answer. Once you have come up with one or two, go online or to your library together, and research that person. You may find and read a biography together or the person may currently be in the news.

Peyton's Point of View
To me a hero is someone who is nice to people, who helps people, who stands up for people and stands up for herself. George Washington is one of my heroes because he was the leader against King George III and he helped win the Revolutionary War and then became our first president. He helped a lot of people and he was very nice and kind and he wanted the best for the people.

Questions for Reflection:
1. What do you admire most about a particular person?
2. What challenges did/do they face in their lives and how do/did they handle it/them?
3. What kind of people do you think they had/have around them to support them?

4. How do/did others in their lives react to them?
5. Were they popular or were they rejected for a stand they took on an issue?
6. Were/are they seen as a hero by many others or did their actions go mainly unnoticed?
7. Are you like that person in any way? How similar? How different?
8. What could you do today to honor them or their memory?

Making a Difference in Our World

From a very early age, children can be a part of making our world a better place. The idea that we are stewards of the earth and can be a part of the Creator's continuing act of creation here on earth is an ancient concept at the core of many faiths such as Judaism, Islam, Buddhism and Christianity. "To whom much is given, much is required," is a quote from Luke 12 in the New Testament. While we may debate whether we qualify to be in the category of having been given "much," if you have an education and enough money to buy this book, you've got more materially than most people in the world. It is our responsibility to give something of our time, energy or resources for the greater good. In return, there are great rewards: a sense of self-esteem, well-being, connection with others, and generosity of spirit, to name a few.

Volunteerism

Giving back is an idea promoted in our popular culture. In Scouting, children are taught that service is central to self-empowerment and leadership. In school, children are encouraged to give back through service projects. For some children, the idea is innate, and others need some encouragement and modeling from parents.

Volunteering your time takes a commitment and sacrifice, but it is worth it. Dr. Albert Schweitzer, the famed theologian, philosopher, and physician once said, "I don't know what your destiny will be;

but one thing I do know: the only ones among you who will be really happy are those who have sought and found how to serve."

You can volunteer on a one-time or regular basis. You can volunteer with the old or the young, or with animals. It doesn't matter. Just do it!

The ideas are endless!

Going Green: How Can We Help Save Our Environment?

During the last decade, the world has awakened to the affects of global warming. Citizens have been encouraged to participate in reducing their carbon footprint through a variety of means. And schools are right on board, educating our younger generation about the impact one person can have in saving the earth. Students want to help.

One local elementary school had some creative ideas about how to think "green." Students collected all the plastic water bottles which the children had used over a week-long period. Then they strung them all together with string and formed a "bottle serpent" which they presented to the student body and wrapped around their whole gymnasium! It raised such awareness of the amount of plastic that they used and threw away each week that the "serpent" went on tour around the region.

Families too have been encouraged to help the "green revolution." Participating in activities at home and around your neighborhood can be fun to do together, plus they help children feel that they are contributing to the larger good. Whether it's picking up trash around a local park or on the streets of your town, families may begin an informal "adopt-a-spot."

Many towns, such as the one where we live, now require residents to recycle certain items out of the trash. We must separate out plastics, aluminum, newspapers and magazines every week. Even though it takes some work for me, it does feel good to know our household is helping in some small ways.

Hearing about the efforts of others is contagious. After telling Peyton about the story I reported about the "bottle serpent," she decided to start taking a refillable water bottle to school every day to do her part in helping the environment. We have also worked on turning off lights, and using less water, all of which can be hard habits to break. Our family car is a hybrid and we use non-toxic cleaners. But there is much more we could do.

How about you?

Peyton's Point of View
A lot of times there are things you can help out with in your school. It makes you feel good that you're helping other people. Maybe one day you'll need help, and people will help you and you'll remember when you used to help people.

When I get older, I want to go with my mom and build houses in Nicaragua like she's done. I also want to go overnight and serve dinner to the homeless in New York City.

Questions for Reflection:
1. What's something you want to know more about or have an interest in? If it's animals, why not volunteer at your local animal shelter to walk the dogs or play with the cats?
2. Who are people that you know in need? How about spending some time collecting food from your neighborhood for your local food pantry and delivering it there?
3. What is something you see that needs doing? How about raking an elderly neighbor's leaves or shoveling their walkway?

4. Is your family doing anything in the effort to help protect our environment?
5. Where do you think you could cut back and help?
6. Do you think it is important to conserve energy?
7. What is one thing your family could change today which could help save the earth?

Outside Forces

Alcohol, Drugs and Cigarettes

In our culture children are bombarded with messages about drugs, both legal and illegal, through the media and entertainment. In the United States there are drugs which are legal, such as alcohol, tobacco and prescription drugs; and those which are illegal, such as marijuana, heroin, and crystal meth. There is also illegal use of products legally bought, such as inhalants and cough syrups.

At some point in their lives some children may decide for one reason or another to experiment on their own or with peers. The questions are: what information do they have; are they going to be responsible in their use; are they children at risk of abuse?

In the United States, it is illegal to sell alcohol to anyone under age 21, and tobacco to anyone under 18 (some states have raised the limit to 19.) Still some young children manage to get these things. Some try substances in their homes. They see their siblings, parents or other family members using them and it encourages them to want to try them, too. Some parents say they want to take the mystique out of alcohol and choose to serve wine or beer on occasion to their young children.

Contrary to popular opinion, according to the National Institute on Drug Abuse (part of the National Institute of Health), most teens do not use marijuana. Annual research shows one in seven tenth graders use marijuana and that number decreases by twelfth grade. They say they do it for a variety of reasons: they see brothers, sisters, friends, even older family members using it; they hear songs about it, see it on TV or in the movies and think it's cool. Some say they use it to escape from problems with school, family or friends. (For more information see www.drugabuse.gov.) Study after study show that if young children use substances, they are likely to continue use into adolescence and beyond. Early intervention beginning in elementary school is key to long term prevention.

As a television news reporter, I love doing feature segments about people whose stories touch the depth of the human experience. I have done several interviews with people who became drug or alcohol addicted early in their lives and later found sobriety through 12 Step programs. Their stories, although different in circumstances all tell of an eventual inability to stop using those substances which once gave them some sort of relief from the pain they experienced.

Peyton and I talked about one woman's story the night I went to New York City to accept an award for that special series. She was curious about it and this is how I tried to explain it.

SW: The woman had an allergy to alcohol. You've seen

what crazy things some people do when they have an allergy to alcohol. They act silly and do things they wouldn't normally do. Sometimes they do things that put them or other people in danger.

PW: How do you know if you have an allergy to alcohol?

SW: Well, it's usually something you're born with. Usually it comes from your parents and they got it from their parents. It comes through your genes. I don't know if your birth parents have that gene and passed it on to you, or not. But if you decide to drink, when you're over age 21, then we would talk about what it makes you feel like. That's one way to tell. That's a long time from now, but it's good to talk about it now.

PW: Why do people drink anyway?

SW: They drink because they like the taste or they like the way it makes them feel. But sometimes people drink to make them feel more comfortable in a situation where they don't feel comfortable and that's when it becomes not so good.

PW: Why?

SW: Because people who have good self-esteem don't need to drink or take drugs to feel comfortable within themselves and to have a good time.

PW: Okay.

Peyton's Point of View
It's horrible to do any of these when you're only a kid. It can hurt you when you're older, too and you can become addicted.

It's not good to be addicted to that kind of stuff because you could really hurt your body and other people around you. Anyway, who would smoke when you're my age? If you feel peer pressure, you should just say, "No." Don't do it and run home. Smoking is really gross, putting that smoke in your body.

Questions for Reflection:
1. What do you think about smoking?
2. What do you know about drug and alcohol use?
3. Do you know anyone who has used or who currently uses any of these substances?
4. If yes, have you seen any trouble associated with their use?
5. Why do you think drugs and underage drinking and smoking are illegal?
6. Why do you think people drink and smoke underage and do drugs?
7. What would you say if someone you like offered you a drink or drugs? (role play)
8. What would you say to someone who offered you a cigarette?
9. (If the parents have alcoholism in their family) Do you understand that our family is especially susceptible to problems with alcohol (an allergy to alcohol) and that means you may also have that issue if you drink or drug?
10. Do you understand that I (the parent) do not want you to drink alcohol under age 21?
11. Do you understand that I (the parent) do not want you to use drugs?
12. Do you understand that I (the parent) do not want you to smoke cigarettes?
13. Do you know that I am here to help you if you ever find yourself in a difficult situation or if someone you know needs help?

Internet Safety: Cyber-bullying and Child Predators

It's a different world today than when we were children. With the Internet so widely available, many children are savvier than we ever dreamed of being. While the Internet is a marvel of technology, it also has a down side, particularly when it comes to children. It's sad to say, but you have to be on the lookout for predators who would take advantage of children as unsuspecting victims. I am *not* a fan of living your life in fear, by any means. However, parents must live with their eyes wide open. We must be conscious. We no longer live in a world where children can play outside all afternoon without checking in with their parents. Now, their world might include going online and communicating with every person who looks at their MySpace or Facebook page, if they have one.

This year I decided to open an email account for Peyton so she could communicate with friends who live in London. I told her that I would be checking her account every week, with her knowledge, and would be putting on parental controls to limit the websites she could visit and sites that could pop up unbeknownst to her.

Two months after I opened the account, she was receiving some emails which I felt were inappropriate. She had been so excited about getting an email account she had asked anyone she knew to email her. After we discussed it, I changed the parental controls to allow into her account only communication with our agreed-upon email addresses. That resolved the situation, at least for now. I realize the rules may change when she gets to Middle School. We also repeated the same conversation again in front of her father so we would all be on the same page.

Cyber-bullying

Cyber-bullying is a form of bullying which can take place 24/7. The National Crime Prevention Council's definition of cyber-bullying is "when the Internet, cell phones or other devices are used to send or post text or images intended to hurt or embarrass another person." StopCyberbullying.org, an organization which watches over Internet safety, security and privacy, defines cyber-bullying as "a situation when a child, tween or teen is repeatedly 'tormented, threatened, harassed, humiliated, embarrassed or otherwise targeted' by another child, tween or teen using text messaging, email, instant messaging or any other type of digital technology."

According to StopCyberbullying.org, the cyberbullying prevention site operated by WiredSafety.org.

For some households this may not be an issue because the child is not online at home, but children these days are learning about the Internet at school. The more parents can educate their children as they are learning, the better. Many children already navigate their way around the web with ease. With the increase of the use of social networking sites such as Facebook and MySpace, elementary school-aged children can be bullied just as easily as teenagers.

And even if a child is not on a computer at home, she can be subject of cyber-bullies just by being aware that a certain website exists that mentions her. She can get email remotely at a friend's house, or a text message. Just knowing a picture has been posted of her can be victimizing.

If your child is active on the web or texting, parents need to be aware and keep up with technology. Talking with your child about the potential pitfalls of cyber-bullying will help set up a climate of open, honest communication in case something hurtful does happen. Kids don't want their parents to "freak out" and make the situation worse for them. They want it just to go away so they can fit in.

It is also important to know the school protocol in regard to "safe" computer use. You can ask school officials if they use monitoring and filtering systems which can also be used at home. Do parents have to sign Internet forms for children's use at the school? And when are they allowed on the computers at school? You can also ask if Internet safety is discussed at school so principles can be reinforced at home.

Child Predators

Many children visit kid-friendly websites. Some sites are suggested by teachers as a way to get used to how the web works and for homework assignments. Others are for recreation, such as clubpenguin.com, webkinz.com, poptropica.com, creaturebreeder. com. Some have chat rooms (for example, poptropica.com and clubpenguin.com) where you can ask questions of other users.

Other sites give children the opportunity to communicate with controlled questions and responses (for example: webkinz.com). In some cases, sites require a parent to join and give permission for admission to her child. Others require that the child be a minimum of twelve years old to join. Children can begin conversations with people without even knowing the person and can inadvertently give information about themselves because they are naïve and don't know that someone on those sites might want to harm them.

I looked at a new site Peyton was on the other day which she had heard about from a friend. They had set up an account without my knowledge, even though you are supposed to be thirteen to participate. She was excited about this site because she was able to watch baby animals grow. She was able to buy eggs, watch them hatch and create a whole personality. When I looked at the site, I felt uneasy. As it turns out, users can "breed" their animals together with other users. All it takes is a request from one to "breed" with another. This may be frivolous, but there was a request from an unknown user to "breed" with Peyton. A bit too over the top for me. We discussed why I was uncomfortable and we decided she didn't need to "breed" with anyone, since she could buy her own eggs online – with pretend money, of course.

Although my daughter rolled her eyes at me during the above discussion, predatory behavior on the Internet is insidious. It attacks in a place where you assume your child is safe — your home. It's no longer as simple as "avoiding the bully on the corner" or "telling a stranger you don't want a ride." Kids want to know what others think about them all of the time, in order to be accepted. They can't help but read or look at damaging emails, texts, pictures, websites, blogs, and so forth. Some of those are places where adults can hang out and watch for the vulnerable to show up.

WHAT CAN I DO?

- Parents need to keep an open communication with their children about online activities.

- Law enforcement officials and child advocates who conduct seminars for parents about cyber-bullying and Internet child safety suggest keeping the computer which your child uses in a family room, rather than in your child's room, so activity can be monitored.

- You can put parental controls on your child's email account and allow access only onto certain websites. Those controls, however, are computer specific and need to be put on each computer to which your child has access.

- If you are concerned about website usage, you can also check the "history" of sites viewed on any computer, although this can be erased by the user.

You may also use a keystroke logger to monitor usage. Keystroke logging allows you to anonymously monitor the strokes used on a keyboard. It can be either software or hardware-based.

Peyton's Point of View

If you don't know someone online, don't talk to them. Don't give your real name, even on kid's sites. Don't say anything personal because you don't want to give that information out. If someone asks you something, just log off. Don't answer, and be sure to tell your parents.

Questions for Reflection: (for parents and children)
1. Have you ever heard of cyber-bullying?
2. Has anyone ever written mean or hurtful things to you on the Internet?
3. If yes, what did they say?
4. Do you know of anyone else who has had someone write mean or hurtful things to them on the Internet?
5. If yes, have they told anyone what happened? Why or why not?
6. What would you do if you suddenly got a mean message from someone?

Music

Music is a universal language. People of every culture make it, play it and sing it to communicate. Music with or without words can take people to another realm of their existence and touch the deepest levels of their spirits.

My parents always said that a person isn't truly educated unless they know music. They took us to the Metropolitan Opera a few times, to the ballet, and other classical music concerts. Music was also part of our home life. I have memories of my father sitting at home on Sunday morning, reading the *New York Times* while listening to operas such as *Tosca* and *La Boheme*, composers such as Chopin and Sibelius, and musicians such as Ferante and Teicher and Al Hirt. Because he loved them, I loved them and the melodies made their way deep into my soul. Listening to music and reading the *Times* together was one way I could bond with my dad – even if the newspaper blocked the view between us!

And my mother is a beautiful singer. She was always singing around the house, bringing joy and beauty to many moments. A melodic "Good morning to you" was one way I was greeted to a new day. Thanks, Mom.

Music seems to help bring good out of the not-so-good. My older sister and I sang while washing dishes and raking what seemed to be endless piles of leaves. Somehow a song made it just a little bit easier. After raking for several hours one time, we even made up our own lyrics to the tune of "These Eyes," the 1968 smash hit by The Guess Who. One line went "I never want to see another leaf in my life again!"

We had the good fortune of learning to play instruments. Violin and piano were my choices, although I hated to practice. My mother finally stopped making me after a while, because I lacked the daily discipline. I now regret having given them up, because as an adult I would love to have the skills.

With the advent of IPods and MP3 players, music has become even more accessible to young children. They don't have to be sitting in their rooms to listen. Peyton and I love listening to music, especially in the car. She is a lyricist and is constantly making up new songs whenever she can. But I also like to listen to music with her so I know what she's taking into her mind.

With devices requiring headphones, parents aren't always aware of the songs to which their children are listening. Determining the age appropriateness of songs is an on-going job. But if parents are able to listen in, songs can be good opportunities for conversation.

One parent says she was surprised when her elementary school-aged child started singing "It's a Bloody Mary Morning" by Willie Nelson. When asked if she knew what a "Bloody Mary" was, she didn't. Nevertheless, she was belting it out proudly for the world to hear. She had heard it on her father's iPod, and liked the tune. The mother says they talked about the alcohol reference and how others probably wouldn't understand why she would be singing about it. Songs with violent or sexual lyrics can affect children and may encourage like behavior if they idolize the singer. Fortunately there have been calls in the music industry worlds of rap, hip-hop, rock, pop, and country for some accountability to curb lyrics which incite destructive behavior. For example, take the popular song by Carrie Underwood called, "Before He Cheats." The woman in the song is destroying her lover's car, because she's mad he cheated on her. Do you want your child singing that song and thinking that behavior is appropriate?

Then there are sexual lyrics and images. Music videos are as popular as ever, and even young stars are sometimes sexed-up. Take for example the controversy over Miley Cyrus wearing short-shorts and sliding up and down a pole, making her look like a pole dancer. There have been other scandals in the national news where she was deemed over-the-top sexy. Although Billy Ray has defended his daughter, and she has apologized to her fans, the images are left in young girls' and boys' minds.

Of course, songs can bring encouragement and inspiration too. Miley's popular song, "It's the Climb" is a perfect example. The song is about how life lessons come during the journey and not necessarily at the destination. While the song may roll off the lips of children who like the tune and singer, there are great life lessons to be discussed.

Peyton's Point of View

Playing an instrument in an orchestra helps me learn about harmony. All the sounds come together. I love listening to music too. I love Lady Gaga, Taylor Swift, Bon Jovi, Kids Bop, Ashley Tisdale, Selena Gomez, Demi Lovado, Phinneas and Ferb. I also like to make up my own songs.

Why do some songs have bad words? It's just not fair that some parents then don't let their kids listen to them. That's why Kid's Bop is good because they take out all the bad words.

Questions for Parents:
1. Do you have guidelines in your house about what music is age-appropriate for your children?
2. If you don't, have you considered any?
3. Do you periodically look at your child's iPod to see what's on it?
4. Do you ever talk about the lyrics with your child?

Questions for Parents and Children:
1. What is your favorite type of music?
2. Who's your favorite artist?
3. What's your favorite song right now? Why?
4. Do you think that musical lyrics affect how people behave?
5. How do music videos affect your opinions of the artists?
6. What does this song mean to you?
7. What's it about?
8. Do you think the song is appropriate just because it doesn't have curse/bad worse in it?
9. When would a clean song be appropriate?

Television

What are your child's favorite television shows? Have you ever sat and watched those shows together? Do you know what the characters do and say on them?

I had to limit the shows my daughter was watching when one day she responded to an adult at our church. In her sassiest voice, she said, "I don't think so…" while waving her finger in the air. I looked back at her and said, "Oh no, *I* don't think so." That response had gotten a laugh on TV, but to an unrelated audience, it wasn't funny! I knew exactly where she had seen it and explained to her how others might hear it. I knew she hadn't meant it in the way it sounded and she seemed surprised when I stopped her. After all, she was just parroting back what she had seen and heard from someone she liked on television. And that was on the Disney Channel, no less!

A while back, we had a discussion after Peyton saw a picture of Jamie Lynn Spears on the cover of a grocery store tabloid. She's the actress who played Zoey on Nickelodeon's *Zoey 101*. Peyton was upset because the show was going to be discontinued. That's because Jamie Lynn, Brittney Spear's little sister, got pregnant at age sixteen in real life! The network didn't think she would be a good role model for young children. Nevertheless, Peyton thought that move was unfair. She wanted to see a continuation of the plot of the story.

> SW: Why were you bummed when you found out *Zoey 101* wasn't going to be on anymore?
>
> PW: Because the show couldn't be on any more.
>
> SW: Why?
>
> PW: Because she got pregnant.
>
> SW: What does that mean?
>
> PW: It means she's having a baby. They thought it would be too inappropriate for her to do the show.
>
> SW: Why is it inappropriate?
>
> PW: Because she has a big belly.
>
> SW: Do you think Zoey is a good role model?
>
> PW: No.

SW: Why not?

PW: Because, it's good that she likes her boyfriend, but she shouldn't do that because she had a career and now she can't go to college and she has to get married.

SW: She can go to college down the road, but she'll have a little baby too. What do you think that says to other little girls who look at her as a role model?

PW: That they should get a baby when they're young.

SW: And what do you think about that?

PW: I don't think that it's good because you have to be able to actually live life.

SW: What does that mean?

PW: You need to be able to go on a roller coaster, and go bungee jumping or do stuff before you get in a real relationship.

SW: What do you think Zoey is feeling?

PW: I think she feels bad because all of the kids all over the world who love *Zoey 101* can only watch the shows that they have watched before…the ones that are on over and over again.

Different households have different rules about the type of shows and amount of television they allow in their homes. Some people allow unlimited access to young children at any hour, while others don't even have a television. But most of us fall somewhere in between. What guidelines have you set in your house?

Try This:

- Watch your child's favorite shows with them.
- Discuss the dialogue together. How are the characters treating each other?
- Change the channel if you don't like what is going on, after explaining why.
- Set parental controls on your television.
- Limit the amount of television in your house.
- Communicate your guidelines to all caregivers.

Peyton's Point of View

I like *SpongeBob, Wizards of Waverly Place*, and *Sandboy and Chum Chum*. The good thing about TV is you get ads for toys – okay, maybe that's a bad thing!

You can get facts on the TV. And my mom's on the TV, what could be bad? The bad thing is a lot of kids get addicted to it. I have picked up some bad habits from it. You can tell a show is not appropriate when it's all sassy and has "attitude."

Questions for Reflection:

1. What is your favorite show on TV?
2. Do your friends watch it, too?
3. What's happening on this show these days?
4. Who are the characters and how do you think they are viewed by their friends on the show?
5. Why do you like the characters?
6. Do you know anyone in your life like the character you most like?
7. Do you want to be like him or her?
8. How do they get along with their parents on the show?
9. What kinds of things so they talk about?
10. What makes a television show appropriate?
11. Do you think a show is appropriate just because they don't use curse/bad words?

Contemporary Stories

Reflecting on a story together is an effective way to get conversation going with your child. It can also stimulate imagination. Stories are used in all world religions and cultures. Sometimes it is easier for people to hear truths taught by stories rather than being told directly. Here are a few examples.

Blessing or Curse? - Folk Tale

There was a man who lived in a remote village. He owned a beautiful horse. The villagers would often visit him and say, "How fortunate you are to have such a horse; you must be a happy man."

"Perhaps," the man said." But what seems like a blessing may be a curse." Well, the villagers thought that was a crazy thing for him to say given his obvious good fortune, until one day the horse broke out of its corral and got away.

"What a terrible thing that has happened to you," said the villagers to the man. "How unfortunate you are."

"Perhaps," said the man. "But what seems like a curse may well be a blessing."

Well, the villagers thought the man was truly mad, until one day the horse returned bringing with it a whole herd of wild horses, which by law now belonged to the man.

"What good fortune has befallen you," said the villagers. "How blessed you are to have all these horses."

"Perhaps," said the man. "But what seems like a blessing may be a curse." The villagers could not understand how the man could say such a thing, until one day when the man's only son was riding one of the new stallions fell off and broke his leg.

"Oh what terrible misfortune," said the villagers. "If only you had never seen those horses."

"Perhaps," said the man. "But what seems like a curse may be a blessing." The villagers could not understand how the man could say such a thing until one day the king rode through the village and drafted every able-bodied young man to fight a terrible war in the north. All young men of the village were killed except the man's son who was unable to go to war because of his broken leg.

And so to this day, in that village, the people still say, "What seems like a blessing may be a curse and what seems like a curse may be a blessing."

Questions for Reflection:
1. Have you ever experienced something that seemed really sad at first, but then turned out to be a good thing?
2. Have you ever experienced something that seemed great and then turned out to be difficult?
3. Is it important to reserve judgment?

The Leather Man -- a true story

This story is about a mysterious traveler known only as the "Leather Man." He wandered day after day during the 1800's and was given his name because all he wore was a suit made of leather – a suit that probably weighed over sixty pounds! One of the strange things about this man is that even though he never spoke to anyone, he was known by all he encountered. You see, he traveled the same 365 mile loop through parts of Western Connecticut and southern New York every year. In fact, his route was so predictable that people are said to have set their clocks to the timing of his visits. And people along his path would offer him food, tobacco, and drink.

He had no home except caves he found along his way. Some are still regularly visited in Ward Pound Ridge, Bedford Hills, and Yorktown in Westchester County in New York, and in parts of Connecticut. There is a tombstone in his honor in a cemetery right off Route 9 in Scarborough, NY. The only way to find them all is to ask local people who follow his history.

The Leather Man's legacy is kept alive by people who tell his story and who continue to try and figure out who he really was. He has been sung about by rock group Pearl Jam, and researched by historians, but everyone who has had any kind of exposure to the haunting mystery of this man, including Peyton and me, is drawn to know more about him and his purpose here.

Note: If you ever get a chance, it's worth tracking down some of these caves. Peyton and I have been to three of them in Westchester County, NY and Connecticut.

Questions for Reflection:
1. Why do you think the Leather Man never spoke?
2. What do you think he would say if he ever did say anything?
3. What do you think it would it be like to travel around and live in caves?
4. It is said the Leather Man carried a prayer book around with him. What do you think he prayed for?

The Christmas Menorahs: How a Town Fought Hate by Janice Cohn; also in a play form, Paper Menorahs
This is another true story which took place in 1993 in Billings, Montana. Isaac Schnitzer belonged to one of the few Jewish families in town. One night Isaac was startled when a huge rock was thrown through his bedroom window on the third night of Hanukkah. It broke his menorah.

The police came and talked to Isaac's parents and encouraged them to take down their holiday decorations to avoid further vandalism. Chief Inman explained that there had been some similar hateful acts against people of different groups, such as African-Americans and Native Americans. Isaac couldn't believe someone would do this just because he was Jewish and he was scared about putting the menorah back up in his window.

When people in town tried to find out who was responsible, they began to learn about the meaning of Hanukkah to Jews.

One woman suggested that other town members put menorahs up in their windows too. Churches joined in the idea too. Soon the whole town had menorahs in their windows. Isaac was so overwhelmed, he decided it was time to put his menorah back up, too.

Questions for Reflection:
1. Why do you think people do acts of hate against other groups?
2. Why did others in the town put up menorahs even though they weren't Jewish?
3. What do you think it meant to them to do such a gesture?
4. What do you think it meant to Isaac and his family to see all of the menorahs?
5. Have you ever been different from others around you? What was it like?

Using the Headlines as Teachable Moments

Children see and overhear the news in the media. They are aware of events, even if we don't think they are. If you keep the details at an age-appropriate level, you can use news events as opportunities to talk with your child.

Here are some things to keep in mind:

- Know the story yourself before you talk about it.
- Decide how much information you want to share. What is age-appropriate?
- Decide when you will talk about it. Some families discuss current events at the dinner table, others when the story is heard.
- Debrief the feelings in each story and determine how your child is relating the story to their own lives. Are they scared the same thing will happen to them, for example?
- Talk about all different kinds of stories, so there is a sense that all news is not bad news.
- Know when to stop. Children will let you know when they've heard enough because they will be satisfied with what you've told them. You don't need to tell them everything.
- At times it is appropriate to *turn off the television*.

Here are a few examples of stories which hit the news cycles and provided a way to talk about current events while still being age-appropriate.

Tragic Accidents

In July 2009, there was a horrible car accident just north of New York City in which eight people were killed. Four of the dead were small children. Toxicology reports revealed that the driver had a blood alcohol level two times the legal limit and had been smoking pot close to the time of the accident. The woman responsible killed herself, four of the five children in her minivan and three other men in the SUV which she hit head on.

We happened to be away at the time of the accident, but we saw coverage of the scene on national news when we were in the airport. Since it was near where we lived, I felt I needed to address the situation in some way. I simply told Peyton, "There was a very bad car crash in which four children and four adults died." "Why?" she asked. "Because they think the driver had been drinking alcohol and taking drugs." And we left it at that. I didn't need to tell her any of the gory details. That would have been more than she could handle. Local news stations covered the story for quite some time and I made sure to turn it off when she was present.

Questions for Reflection:
1. What did you hear about the incident?
2. How did it make you feel when you heard about it?
3. Sometimes stories are too difficult for young children understand. Is there anything more you need to know about this story?

Racism

Right after the attacks of 9/11, a Sikh Gudwara, or place of worship, was burned in upstate New York. Sikhs are from India and they comprise the fifth largest religion in the world. The men often wear turbans on their heads and sometimes have been mistaken for Muslims, especially after pictures of Osama Bin Laden began to show up on television screens everywhere.

After an investigation, several teens were arrested for the burning of the temple Gobind Sadan. They thought they were burning a mosque, where Muslims worship, which in their minds had some connection with Osama Bin Laden because of the similar sound of the name. There was, of course, no connection.

When the teens came before the judge, members of the Sikh community came and asked the judge for leniency in the sentencing.

Questions for Reflection:
1. What do you think made the teens burn down a house of worship, other than the name?
2. Why do you think the Sikh community wanted to forgive the teens?
3. Have you ever been forgiven for something you don't think you deserved?
4. What kind of impact do you think the action of the Sikhs had on the teens? On the rest of the town?

The Financial Crisis of 2007-2009

The economic crisis involving failed banks and lending institutions, government takeovers, massive amounts of foreclosures, millions of jobs lost, and countless dollars in savings washed away, led many to think that we were in a time similar to the Great Depression. There were countless news stories on national and local stations which covered this, along with the reality of reduced school, and family budgets as well.

Questions for Reflection:
1. Talk about your family's situation and how the financial crisis affected you. Did you cut back on spending, save more, or do something else?
2. When you hear that banks are closing and people are losing their homes and jobs, what are your concerns?
3. Do you know anyone's parents who have been affected by losing their job or home?
4. Do you worry about our family financially as a result of this story?
5. There are many smart people doing what they can to make sure it turns around, but how does this situation make you feel about the future?

Peyton's Point of View
Some of the news stories are inappropriate for kids. They contain

shootings, alcohol, drugs, and other stuff. I don't think about them, but I think some other kids do. I hear them talking about the stories, like someone just got shot or car crashes. But the good news is there's good news. Like the Yankees winning the World Series is good news. You don't have to watch the bad news. Overhearing stories make you curiouser and make you want to hear more. That's not good because you're just a little kid. You shouldn't have to be worrying about that stuff.

Movies: Ratings and Reviews

Going to the movies is a great American pastime. When I was a child, the only place to see a movie was in a theatre. Now we can rent movies, download them, own them, and watch them on personal DVD players or computers. Wow, just saying that makes me feel old!

Along with movie technology, the substance in them has changed as well. Digital effects, increased violence, more intense plots all have created what I call the need for a bigger "WOW Factor." That means it takes more to get us thrilled, scared, or engaged in a movie. No longer does the excitement and violence of a "Roadrunner" cartoon suffice. Now young children are exposed to "amped up" movie violence where engaging guinea pigs are commandoes out to save the world. (*G-Force* is a Disney film that topped box office revenues during its first few weeks after release in the summer of 2009.)

As we experience more, we become accustomed to more, and we expect more. So where does this leave our children when it comes to what is age-appropriate and what they actually will want to see at the movies?

One grandmother wanted to take her third grade granddaughter to a G-rated movie which had gotten great reviews. "That's a baby movie," the girl said. The problem is that the girl had been going to adult movies with each of her divorced parents. Her mom had taken her to an action film rated PG-13. Her father took her to see a romantic comedy which was rated "R" due to sexual content and language. Both were popular movies at the box office. When asked how she liked the movies, the little girl replied, "I don't know, I missed most of it because I had my hands over my eyes."

Many of us push the envelope with movies and our kids. I remember taking Peyton to her first movie just before she was three years old. I thought it would be appropriate because it was about dogs and sledding. It was a great movie for a seven-year-old, but I realized it was too loud and the action too fast for a child her age. My clue was that she cried when it got too loud. I must admit, my motive was totally selfish. I wanted to see the movie and wanted Peyton to be old enough to see it too. Wrong move.

Movies have ratings for a reason. In 1968 the Motion Picture Association of America began rating movies as a way to warn viewers about a film's content. While adherence is voluntary, most local theatres will not show a movie which is not rated (unless it's an art, classic, or indie film.) These are the designations as of 2009:

G: General Audiences. All ages admitted. These are family films and you can be guaranteed there is no issue with language, violence, or sexual activity or innuendo.

PG: Parental Guidance Suggested. Some material may not be suitable for children under age ten. They may contain mild language, crude humor, thematic elements, sexual themes, scary moments and/or violence. There will be no drug content, but you may find a few racial insults. Older movies with a PG rating might now be classified as PG-13; an example is *Airplane* where there is strong sexual references and some nudity.

Unfortunately, movies these days don't seem to make as much money if they don't have something controversial in them, so what might have been "G" movies long ago are now made into PG and PG-13 movies. For example, the Harry Potter series as "G" rated movies just wouldn't have the same draw if they didn't have some of the darkness and action scenes which demand a PG rating. Take the PG rated *Harry Potter and the Half-Blood Prince*. The movie's website says it received that rating because of scary images, some violence, language, and mild sensuality.

PG-13: Parents Strongly Cautioned. In 1984 the PG rating was split, since there seemed to be a broad range of films in this category. In order to give parents more information as to the intensity of a film, a new rating was instituted, PG-13, which meant parental guidance suggested for children under the age of 13. When a film has drug use, it requires a rating of at least PG-13. *G.I. Joe: The Rise of the Cobra*, out in the summer of 2009, was heavily advertised on Nickelodeon, which targets kids of young ages. Yet this movie, named after an action figure doll, is not appropriate for younger children. The PG-13 rating is due to "strong sequences of action violence and mayhem throughout." That's an understatement. I saw this movie and was almost "high" on adrenaline after sitting through all of the violence. Teens would be able to handle this movie, but younger children, no way. It has a rating of PG-13 for a good reason.

R: Restricted. Anyone under seventeen must be accompanied by an adult guardian. Movies in this category may contain some adult material, such as "adult themes, adult activity, hard language, intense or persistent violence, sexually-oriented nudity, drug abuse, or other elements; parents are counseled to take this rating very seriously." In fact the MPAA website actually says, "Generally, it is not appropriate for adults to bring their young children with them to R-rated movies."

It is interesting to me how many parents go into the theater, buy tickets for their young teens to "R" rated movies and then leave them alone to watch by themselves. Many young teens want to see popular action movies with an "R" rating, but they may also get a dose of drugs and sex along with it. Parents may not even know what content their children are watching. What's the deal?

NC-17: No one 17 and under is admitted; often designated for erotic material. Most movie houses know these films are not profitable, so they edit and release them under the R rating.

Peyton's Point of View
I have seen some inappropriate movies. When my parents were out of town, my babysitter let me watch *Poseidon* and *Little Miss Sunshine*. (Both are R-rated.) Whoops! I watch some PG-13 movies. They're okay sometimes. I like kids' movies that are funny, scary, and crazy.

Movie Reviews
While there are far too many movies out to review, we've included a few which we believe are worthy of watching by elementary school-aged students and their parents.

The Ultimate Gift (2007, Fox Faith Films.) 1 hour 57 minutes; Rated PG (for some thematic elements, language, some violence); older elementary school through adult.
Themes: redemption, death (death of a child), altruism, grace, entitlement and materialism, values.
Starring: James Garner, Abigail Breslin, Brian Dennehy, Drew Fuller, Ali Hillis, Bill Cobbs

Synopsis:
This is the story of a billionaire patriarch named Red, who dies at the beginning of the film. His grown children greedily gather for the

reading of his last will and testament, but nothing can satisfy them. It is obvious that their relationships with their deceased father have been difficult, and that there is no love lost between them.

Red's grandson, Jason, is a trust-fund baby and as cynical as they come, but he is invited to do a series of tasks told through video-taped messages before he can get what his grandfather calls "The Ultimate Gift." Jason reluctantly ventures on the first of many excruciating journeys, designed to see if he is a man worthy of receiving more.

This is an excellent movie that is rich with possibilities for discussion for older elementary school-aged children through adults. It deals with issues of entitlement in a profound way.

Questions for Reflection:
1. How did you see Jason change throughout the movie?
2. How did his relationship with his grandfather and his father affect the way he saw the world?
3. Why do you think Jason's grandfather chose those particular gifts?
4. Do you think those are important gifts to have in your life? How are they present right now or not present for you, or can you think of people in your life for whom those gift are present?
5. Which character did you like the most and why?
6. How do each character's dreams come true?
7. What would you do if you had all that money?

Holes (2003 Walt Disney Pictures); based on the adventure novel by Louis Sachar; 1 hour 51 minutes; Rated PG (for mild language, difficult themes, violence).
Themes: friendship, altruism, the triumph of good over evil, interracial relationships, racism, murder, unjust treatment of children, friendships among boys.
Starring: Shia LeBoef, Sigourney Weaver, Jon Voight, Patricia Arquette.

Synopsis:
Things just don't go right for Stanley Yelnats. He always seems to be in the wrong place at the wrong time. Stanley is unfairly sentenced to months of detention at Camp Green Lake in Texas for a crime he didn't commit. He and the other boys have to dig holes in the ground for the deceitful warden (Weaver) and her bumbling helpers, Mr. Sir, and Mr. Pendanski. They eventually discover that they are working against an ancient family curse. (This is a good movie to watch with mature children. My daughter's third grade class watched it and discussed it.)

Questions for Reflection:
1. Why did people have such a hard time with Sam and Kate dating?
2. Do you think that was right? Why or why not?
3. What does your Mom/Dad think?
4. Did the digging holes build character? How?
5. Have you, or anyone you know ever been unjustly accused of something?
6. How did they handle it?
7. What do you think about the friendship between Stanley and Hector?
8. Have you ever seen an adult treat children badly? What happened?
9. Do you think there's such a thing as a curse/blessing that can last for generations?
10. How did Stanley earn the respect of the other boys?
11. What do you think about the adults in this film? Did the boys respect them?
12. Do you have any legends in your family?

Mr. Magorium's Wonder Emporium (2007 20th Century Fox) 94 min; Rated G, for younger elementary children;
Themes: creativity, loss/death, living your dreams.

Starring: Dustin Hoffman, Natalie Portman, Jason Bateman, Zach Mills.

Synopsis:
Mr. Magorium (Hoffman) owns and runs a unique and magical toy store. As he draws near to the end of his life, he decides to give his store to his assistant, Molly Mahoney (Portman). In order to transfer ownership, he hires an accountant (Bateman) who is unimaginative and unable to see the magic in the store. No one wants Mr. Magorium to leave, including the items in the store, which throw a temper tantrum. Together, the people who value Mr. Magorium's legacy figure out what it takes to see the magic around and inside of them and reach their dreams.

Questions for Reflection:
1. What would you choose to play with in the store?
2. What affect did the store have on people?
3. What happened to Henry in the movie?
4. Is there some sparkle that's trying to get out of you?
Remember what Mr. Magorium said? "Your life is an occasion. Rise to it!" Go for it!

Kit Kittredge: An American Girl (2008 New Line Cinema); 100 minutes; Rated G; mid elementary school ages and up;
Themes: poverty, discrimination, perseverance, friendship, loss, peer pressure.
Starring: Abigail Breslin, Chris O'Donnell, Juliette Ormond, Stanley Tucci, Joan Cusack, Jane Krakowski.

Synopsis:
This story takes place during the Depression in Cincinnati, Ohio. Along with other families, Kit's family is hit hard by the bad economy. Her father loses his job and has to temporarily leave town to find other work. She and her mother open their home to boarders. Hard times don't diminish Kit's creativity and dreams. Her skills as an investigative reporter help her and her friends solve a mystery of who is behind a string of recent burglaries.

Questions for Reflection:
1. How does Kit keep her dream of being a journalist alive, even when she is told it can't be done?
2. What kind of dreams do you have? What kind of obstacles, if any, do you face in reaching them?
3. Kit faced a lot of teasing from children in her class when her father lost his job. How did she handle it?
4. How do you face other children who tease you at school? Who do you turn to?
5. How did Kit's friends help her solve the crime?
6. How do you and your friends work together?
7. Have you ever missed someone like Kit and her friend missed their fathers?

Other excellent American Girl movies include:
Samantha: An American Girl Holiday, which deals with themes of adoption, classism, friendship, and social issues such as women's voting rights and child labor laws.
Molly: An American Girl on the Homefront, which deals with issues of war, family, service, sacrifice, friendship.

Bridge to Teribithia (2007, Disney) 96 Minutes, Rated PG (due to mature subject matter; older elementary-school ages); based on the Newberry Award-winning book by Katherine Paterson; **Themes:** imagination, bullying, friendship, death/loss, father/son relationship.
Starring: Josh Hucherson, Anna Sophia Robb, Zooey Deschanel.

Synopsis:
Leslie Burke and her family move to town in the middle of the school year. She becomes friends with Jess Aarons at school. Both of them are twelve when they have dealings with school bullies. Through use of their artistic talents and imaginations, they create a magical world full of giants and ogres together. That world ends up helping them face their own giants: loss and bullies.

Note for parents: This movie is very well done, however it deals with the death of one of the main characters. My daughter saw this film in third grade and didn't like it because she said it was too sad. However, it deals with real issues kids face, and if your child is able to deal with issues of loss, it can spark great conversation. Another note: read the book too!

Questions for Reflection:
1. Have you ever become friends with someone you didn't like or understand at first?
2. Why do you think Leslie and Jess were such good friends? What do they offer each other?
3. Have you ever had a place like Terabithia? What is your place like and who goes there with you?
4. Leslie tells Jess, "You are who you are, not your parents." How are you like/not like your parents?
5. Why do you think Jess and his dad have a hard time connecting?
6. How do you connect with your Mom and Dad?
7. How is Jess' relationship with his family different from Leslie's?
8. How does their imagination help them in their real lives?
9. Do you know anyone like Janice or the boys who are bullies?
10. How do they manage to pull off their bullying?
11. What would happen if kids stood up to them?
12. What is it that helps Jess and Leslie finally stand up to those who bully them?
13. How do Jess and Leslie view God differently?
14. Have you ever had a teacher with whom you connected, like Jess does with Miss Edmonds?

The Wild Thornberry's Movie (2002, Nickelodeon/Paramount). 85 minutes; Rated PG (for some adventure peril); mid-elementary-school age and up;
Themes: overcoming injustice; heroism; altruism; mysticism; fulfilling one's destiny; adventure.

Synopsis:
Eliza Dolittle is part of a family of explorers and wildlife filmmakers who travel to exotic lands, this time to the middle of Africa. She is given mystical power by a shaman who enables her to talk to animals and ultimately fulfill her destiny. One day she uncovers a plot by poachers to kill some of her animal friends. As she tries to rescue a cheetah cub, she discovers that some people she thought were friends really aren't. Eliza ends up making a daring rescue of her cheetah cub, as well as saving a herd of a thousand elephants from death.

Questions for Reflection:
1. How does Eliza use her power to help others?
2. Eliza doesn't seem to follow anyone's rules. What do her parents think about this?
3. Do you have a sense of what your destiny is? How does Eliza handle hers?
4. What would it be like to live in the wild like Eliza's family? What do you think you would learn that's different from learning in a classroom?
5. What would you do if someone like Eliza came to your school?
6. What special gifts do you have that can help others?
7. If the animals in your life could talk, what do you think they would say to you?

Video Games

Ever since computers went mainstream, the tech savvy have found a way to play games on them. The video game industry has gone from a small hobby market in the mid-1970's to mainstream in the twenty-first century. Video platforms such as Nintendo, Xbox, Wii, and Playstation are household words for millions of customers of all ages and income brackets. According to the Entertainment Software Association the video gaming industry raked in a whopping 11.7 billion dollars in 2008. That number is growing every year. Parents and kids shell out a few dollars to hundreds of dollars for each game and console.

Parents beware: some games are controversial. As the boundaries have been pushed for how much violence, racism and sexism should be allowed, regulations have been put into place. The Entertainment Rating Software Board, or ESRB, was established in 1994 to help consumers know the content and suitability of video games.

The current ratings according to the ESRB website are:
EC or Early Childhood: Suitable for ages three years and up; usually educational in content. These games contain no material which parents would find inappropriate.
E or Everyone: Video content may be suitable for ages six and older; titles in this category may contain minimal cartoon, fantasy or mild violence, and/or infrequent use of mild language.
E10 or Everyone 10 and older: Titles in this category may contain more cartoon, fantasy or mild violence, mild language, and/or minimal suggestive themes.
T or Teen: Titles have content for ages thirteen and older. Games may include violence, suggestive themes, crude humor, minimal blood, simulated gambling, and/or infrequent use of strong language.
M or Mature: Content may be suitable for ages seventeen and older. Titles in this category may contain intense violence, blood and gore, sexual content, and/or strong language.
AO or Adults Only: Titles with this rating should be played by adults age eighteen and over. These games may have long scenes of intense violence, and/or graphic sexual content and nudity.
RP or Rating Pending: Titles submitted to the ESRB for rating usually before release.
For more information, go to www.esrb.org.

Just because the ratings are clearly marked on the boxes, doesn't mean that children, parents or store clerks abide by them.

One video store owner told me, "If I refused to sell an **M** game (Mature rating) to a kid under seventeen, I'd be out of business in a week." That means that he sells games to young kids that may have cop killings, women who are beaten and "pimped," all sorts of racially charged language, or overt usage of alcohol and drugs. The scary thing is the owner says he will sell to a child under seventeen only with permission of his parents. Wait … that means the kids are getting permission from their parents! What's wrong with this picture?

Many parents have a dilemma. They express frustration with the inability to communicate with a child who is glued to the screen and joystick. They are concerned that the attachment to an elaborate fantasy world will also cripple their child's ability to interface with real people. On the other hand, video games are great time fillers. For children who have high energy, time on their hands, and can't be physically active in the moment, games fill a need.

Then there's another issue – even if you may have certain restrictions on usage and titles in your house, when your child goes to a friend's house, those parents may have different guidelines. One mom says her third grader had a play date which lasted nearly twelve hours. When she picked up her son, he was very agitated and even tried to kick and bite her. Turns out, it had been a rainy day and they had been playing video games the entire time. She was convinced that he was on an adrenaline rush from gaming for so long.

Psychologists agree. Their research shows that "playing a lot of violent video games is related to having more aggressive thoughts, feelings, and behaviors." (Anderson & Bushman, 2001). "Furthermore, playing violent games is also related to children being less willing to be caring and helpful towards their peers." (Anderson et al, under review; Gentile et al., 2004) They say the problem is, "Children spend a great deal of time with violent video games at exactly the ages that they should be learning healthy ways to relate to other people and to resolve conflicts peacefully. Because video games are such good teachers, it is critical to help parents, educators, and policy-makers understand how to maximize their benefits while minimizing potential harms."

The answer is not to ban the games. That's unreasonable in this day and age. Rather, a parent needs to be on top of what her child is playing and to use it in moderation. The American Psychological Association or APA says parental involvement can help lessen the negative effects of video gaming on children. "Psychologists have found that when parents limit the amount of time as well as the types of games their children play, children are less likely to show aggressive behaviors (Anderson et al., under review; Gentile et al., 2004). Other research suggests that active parental involvement in children's media usage, including discussing the inappropriateness of violent solutions to real life conflicts, reducing time spent on violent media, and generating alternative non-violent solutions to problems, all can reduce the impact of media violence on children and youth (Anderson et al., 2003).

From Violent Video Games – Psychologists Help Protect Children from Harmful Effects http://www.apa.org/research/action/games.aspx. ©2004 by the American Psychological Association. Adapted with permission. No further reproduction or distribution is permitted without written permission from the American Psychological Association.

Different parents handle this issue differently. One dad says he and his wife have each game catalogued in their house. Since their three sons are of varying ages, they are allowed to take only age-appropriate games to their own rooms. No cross-over is allowed. When the boy finishes playing that game, he gives it back to his parents for storage.

Another mom told me of her dilemma. Her husband is in the military. They have differing views over what video games their two sons in fifth and sixth grades can play. She says some war games don't show actual killings of people, but you see the blood after the fact. Her husband has a different perspective and doesn't see the harm in those games. Yet, their fifth grader has nightmares at times after playing the games. Mom says she monitors it all carefully and makes sure her boys get outside for sports to work it out physically.

The ESRB website lists over 18,000 individual video games and lists the publisher, rating, content description and platform of each for reference. The key is to know what your child is playing and talk about it.

Try This:
- If you haven't done so yet, set guidelines appropriate for your family. What is the time limit? What ratings are appropriate for each age of your children?
- Do your own experiment. Keep a log of what happens after your child plays a particular video game. Does he seem more aggressive after playing for a time? Talk together about what you see.
- Let your children's friends' parents know before a play date what your guidelines are.
- Get to know the video store management where you shop and let them know your guidelines. You can always change them as your child matures.

Peyton's Point of View
They're good and fun, but it's not good for a kid's brain to play them every day. The vessels in your brain can pop out of your head if you do! You can get so addicted to it you can't move your legs any more. Kids that play all the time are crazier – you can see foam coming out of their mouths! A lot of people who are addicted to them say they're not affected by the games, but they really are. You can see it. But I understand. I play my DS and it's just so much fun that you don't want to stop. If people don't stop me, I won't stop.

Questions for Reflection:
1. What are your favorite video games currently? Why?
2. What games do your friends play?

3. Do you notice anything different in your behavior after you play for a while?
4. How do the characters resolve conflicts in the games you like?
5. Are there stereotypes according to gender and race? How about other cultures?
6. Who are the good guys/bad guys?
7. How are authority figures such as police or soldiers portrayed?
8. How is life in video games different from real life?
9. What actions are inappropriate for you to experience in a game? Why are they inappropriate?
10. If you are playing at a friend's house, and they have a game which we have agreed is not appropriate, what would you do?
11. How can I support you in keeping our guidelines?

The Big Stuff

Feelings Wheel

Knowing what you are feeling on any given day can be a challenge if you're not used to it. Many of us grew up in homes where we didn't put words on feelings. Sure, we felt anger, frustration, joy or peace in different situations, but the open talking about feelings is more of a modern phenomenon, depending upon the household. Knowing what you are feeling and talking about those feelings are skills which must be practiced, just like anything else. It can be difficult for people of any age.

One afternoon after I picked up Peyton from school, I needed to make a business call. I was nervous about it. It was the type of call that I could easily take her to, and if successful, it could have helped my business greatly. Still somewhat new in that business, I felt insecure. While we waited for the customer to arrive at her store, we went to a local park. I was busy trying to figure out what I was going to say to my potential customer. Meanwhile, Peyton was asking me to swing her around. "I need to concentrate on my business stuff right now," I barked back. As soon as I heard myself, I realized how wrong it was to waste this moment. So I put down my things and we played for a bit and shared a laugh. It was only then that I figured out what I was feeling and that I needed to tell her why I had reacted so strongly.

SW: I'm really nervous about this business call. (I had my arm around her while walking back to the car.)

PW: What's the worst thing that could happen, Mom?

SW: You're right – the worst thing she can say is 'No.' I guess I'm afraid of being rejected. Do you have any advice?

PW: Just go in there and be yourself. You'll do great! And if she doesn't want your product, it doesn't mean she doesn't like you.

SW: Thank you, my love. You have helped me so much.

The woman wasn't there when we arrived. She also didn't return my call later on. But my wise daughter told me before bed,

PW: Maybe she's not the right one for your business, Mom. Or, maybe she didn't get home in time.

SW: It's okay, sweet. I am fine and my business will be fine. Thank you for your help.

Out of the mouths of babes comes such wisdom. I was so proud of her. And of me too – I modeled for her that showing your feelings doesn't necessarily mean you'll fall apart. Asking for help is a good thing – and parents need advice from their kids too. I wanted her to know that I valued her experience and opinion. Our relationship matured and grew stronger that day. I caught another glimpse inside a blossoming young woman who has so much to offer the world. If you're not good at naming what you're feeling, here's a partial list we've developed to get you started:

Mad, sad, glad, happy, grumpy, ecstatic, funny, furious, surprised, scared, super, frustrated, angry, peaceful, serene, loving, crazy, lost, mysterious, unsure, bitter, calm, silly, embarrassed, sick, excited, spooked, secretive, confused, depressed, freaking out, nice, nutty, raw, great, gross, awesome, grateful, ridiculous, tired, spent, powerful, at home, weird, flirty, content, small, left out, lonely, on the spot, creative, witty, humble, like a winner, like a loser, loved, energetic, flexible, disappointed, naughty, joyful. Are there others you would add?

Now What?

Assisting a child to name and feel what he is feeling in a certain situation is essential in healthy development. The next step is to help him resolve those feelings and not stay stuck. Here's how one father brilliantly helped his son:

Eleven-year-old Mark played football on a town league. All of his friends happened to be on a rival team. When the two teams met to play, Mark and his friends made a bet. If his team lost he would have to wear red fingernail polish all day at school. If the other team lost, Mark's friends would have to do the same. Mark felt confident his team, whose motto was "Courage" would win.

Mark's team lost. The next morning, Mark went to his father and complained of a stomach ache. He didn't want to go to school. "Could this be ten percent connected to the fact that you lost the bet and have to wear red fingernail polish to school?" his father asked. Mark thought for a minute. "Maybe fifteen percent," he answered. After talking for a few more minutes, the percentage had gone up to forty. "Let's see what feelings are connected with this," his father said. He opened his hand and pointed his fingers to the ground. "I'm feeling embarrassed, and sad and disappointed," Mark revealed. With each feeling, his dad wiggled a finger. "I get it," Dad said, "but let's connect that to the higher truth here." Then Mark's dad connected the thumb of the hand showing the feelings to the thumb of his other hand, which pointed up to signify the flow of energy from his feelings to the higher truth of the situation. He continued, "What you are actually doing when you follow through with this is honoring your word, yourself and your friendships. It doesn't emasculate you to paint your fingernails. You're a man of your word." Mark thought for a minute. "It makes total sense, Dad"! On the way to school, Mark and his dad stopped at a local drugstore and sat in the car, painting his fingernails bright red. His dad also sent him to school with polish remover just in case he was asked by teachers to take it off. He sent him off with these words, "How do we define courage? It's being afraid, but doing it anyway."

After school Mark's dad waited anxiously at the bus stop. Mark bounded off the bus with a huge smile on his face. "Dad, it was a *great* day!" Mark explained that a teacher had walked by and said, "Cool color," and then asked why he was wearing the polish. Mark explained and the teacher said, "It takes more of a man to wear the polish than *not* to wear the polish." Bingo.

Try This:
Make a Feelings Wheel. You will need cardboard, scissors, pen and a paperclip.
- Take a big piece of cardboard and draw a big circle on it. From the center of the circle, draw lines out to the edge of the circle, like spokes on the wheel of a bicycle.
- Write the feeling words in between each of the lines until you have them all written.
- Cut a small piece of cardboard about three inches long with a point at the end in the shape of an arrow. Take the

paper clip and pierce it through the end of the arrow and then through the middle of the circle, where all the lines converge. Open the paper clip to secure it.
- Take turns closing your eyes and moving the arrow. See where it lands. Then talk about it.

The parent can go first to model that it's okay to share feelings, especially the more difficult ones. For example, say it lands on angry. You might say, "I feel angry when someone cuts me off in traffic." Then you might ask, "When do you feel angry?" Or say it lands on "embarrassed." "Once I was wearing an old pair of underwear underneath my dress, and while walking in front of a room full of people my underwear started to fall down! Have you ever felt embarrassed?"

Making a game out of sharing feelings may open up the space to talk about things that may not come up at other times. It also helps to put words on feelings.

Things I'm Afraid Of

Every human being is afraid of something. Sometimes our fears are real and sometimes they are distorted. When they are distorted, they get bigger or smaller than they should be. Adults can help "right-size" fears with their children so they don't cripple their development.

Many children have a fear of lightning and thunderstorms. That was one of mine. I would awaken and not be able to go back to sleep. That all shifted when my mom sat with me and told me lightning was just God taking a picture with a flash and thunder was the sound of God clapping.

For many children fears seem to come up during the night. Teaching a child to soothe themselves is an important life skill which can be used at any time. I remember lying in my bed at night petrified when I was six years old. My bed was an antique squeaker four feet off the ground. I can still remember making my breath as soft as possible, so I could hear if someone was hiding underneath my bed, waiting to pounce on me once I was asleep. Since I knew sleeping with my parents was not an option, I remember consciously choosing to shift my thoughts to the most beautiful thing I could think of, which at the age of six, was a princess. It was an amazing thing to me to experience how my mood shifted and my fear faded, and lo and behold ... I fell asleep!

Sitting by the side of the town swimming pool at the beginning of the season is a perfect place to hear lots of elementary school-aged children talk about their fears. At our pool, children have to take the deep water test each year until they reach sixteen. That means they can't go off the diving boards until they swim four laps (two lengths of an Olympic sized pool) of the crawl, two laps of backstroke, and tread water for a minute. While that may not seem like much, it seems like a monster feat at the beginning of the season until they literally "get their feet wet" again.

I watched one day as child after child negotiated with their parents over whether they would take the test that day or wait until another day when it didn't seem so scary. The diving boards were beckoning and the squeals of other children were almost irresistible, but not enough to overcome the fear of *"what if I fail?"*

Peyton and I arrived at the pool one day in early June. We had the pool almost completely to ourselves. I said, "Why don't you practice for your swimming test today so you can get it out of the way at the beginning of summer?" The previous evening before bed she had scolded me for asking her if she was planning on taking the test. "You're pressuring me, Mom!" she said. I quickly apologized. But things looked different the next day in the pool. Once she was in the water and trying to do some strokes on her own, it went something like this:

PW: See? I can't do it. (After she tried a few strokes.)

SW: You're scared you won't make it across?

PW: Yes.

SW: Well, let's try it. You did such a good job last year. Do you remember?

(She again tried a few strokes but forgot to breathe.)

PW: See, I can't.

SW: I hear your fear. Sometimes when I'm afraid, I forget to breathe. Let's see if we can get you going and breathing while you're swimming. (I reminded her how she learned to put her face into the water, alternating breathing every other stroke.)

SW: What else do you think you need to get you going? Would goggles help or trying it in the shallow end?

PW: Goggles might help, but I'll stay here in the deep end. (She tried again, and this time she made it across half way.)

PW: Did you see it? I went half of the way! Do you want to watch me?

SW: I am … I am not taking my eyes off of you! (This time she went the whole distance of the pool.)

PW: Did you see how good that was? (She could hardly believe her accomplishment.)

SW: Yes! Are you going to try some more? (Without answering, she tried again and went another whole length.)

Less than an hour later she passed the swimming test. As she watched both boys and girls approach the lifeguard with the same fears about the test, she realized that she wasn't alone. Some of them took it and some didn't, but she was able to be there in support of others who were trying to overcome their own fears.

What if your child is afraid of a parent or caregiver? I grew up with a father who was a rager. Anything could set him off, and we had to walk on the proverbial eggshells to not upset him. Sometimes it was his voice, sometimes all it took was a look to make me tremble. As a child, I didn't know that his anger had nothing to do with me, what I did or did not do. My fear of him and his reactions affected me tremendously by keeping me isolated. I never talked about how afraid I was until I had grown up and left the house. It wasn't until my father was on his deathbed that I was freed of the power my fear of him had over me.

As a child, it would have been healing and empowering for me to talk with someone and acknowledge the truth about the fear I felt of my dad. I don't know if I would have shared my fear, even if I had been given an invitation. Maybe it might have helped if someone had asked, "When dad gets angry, what happens to you? Is there anything you want to say to him?"

Nothing broke my heart as much as to hear my daughter say one day:

> PW: Mom, I'm afraid of you when you yell.
>
> SW: I'm so sorry. I was wrong to yell at you right then. I was afraid and I was angry about something that happened earlier in the day that had nothing to do with you. It was wrong to take it out on you. Please forgive me. Can you tell me about your fear? Was it just this time or are there other times you have been afraid of me?

By talking about it and my owning my fault, it cleared it up right then and there. But every once in a while, I check in with her to hear how she is feeling about something I've said or the tone with which I have spoken. The cycle has to end with me. I don't want her living in fear.

Try This:
Boogeyman Sprays: A friend of mine gave me the idea of using a spray bottle filled with water as a "Boogeyman Spray." You spray the room to ensure that the "boogeyman" or any other threatening creature will not return. I use lightly scented water so that she can smell it and know that it has taken affect. I then leave it in her room, so she has the power to spray it herself, if I am (hopefully) back in bed asleep!

Here's another idea. A friend suggested taking fearful situations and imagining putting them up away on a shelf inside a special "God Box." It's a box that God will take care of. You can relax, knowing the "thing" is always there inside the box, just in case you want it back or you want to take it out to look at it. But in the meantime, God is taking care of it.

Peyton's Point of View
When I think of my fears, I use "the glass half full approach" (see Glass Half Empty or Half Full on page 236). If you face your fears, then maybe they'll be over. Facing your fears is good and having fears is still good. Talking about your fear with someone else would be hard but maybe if they told you their fear and you told them your fear it could be helpful. Having someone supporting you while you're talking about it helps, like saying "It's alright. I have the same fear." Sometimes admitting your fears to your friends makes them think better of you, because they know you have faced them.

Questions for Reflection:

1. What is one thing you are afraid of? (Mom names one, then asks her child to name one.)
2. Look at the fear and right-size it, to keep it in perspective in your life. Pretend to take the fear out of your body and look at it. What does it look like? Is it big or small? Is it ugly and mean- looking or small and sneaky? How does your body feel without it inside? Do you think you could act as if it didn't live inside you?
3. Talk about listening for inner guidance. That means asking, "What is my body telling me about the thing I am afraid of? If I'm really quiet, what is the little voice inside my heart saying to me about how I should respond in this situation?"
4. Do you need an adult's help in this situation?
5. Ask yourself, "Why is this particular thing difficult for me to manage?"
6. "Can I ask for help from friends?" (This helps because it encourages children to listen to their own inner judgment.)
7. What's the worst thing that could happen in the situation/ what's the best outcome? What can I do to help make the better outcome happen?

Gratitude

For years, I have known the importance of making a gratitude list. Recognizing the things for which I am thankful can turn my mind around in an instant when I am feeling the "poor me's." Thanking God for things such as the ability to walk, food to eat, family, and work that is important to me, somehow puts things in the right perspective and makes my heart full and ready to receive more.

There is nothing more unattractive than a child or adult with an attitude of entitlement; the idea that he/she deserves or expects to have something. Of course, there are things to which children *are* entitled: love, safety, respect, and nurturance. If those basic needs are not met, and instead are substituted for acquiring "things", everything gets out of whack. Be very clear, there is no substitute for time, attention and love. (See the movie review of *The Ultimate Gift* on page 210.)

One day Peyton and I went clothes shopping, since the season was changing and last year's clothes no longer fit. Off to the mall we went.

We went to one of Peyton's favorite stores, which had a wide range of "cool" clothes at decent prices. I told her right at the start that we had a budget of $200. My plan was to get enough clothes to bridge her from winter into spring.

Peyton is a great shopper. She goes into a place and immediately knows what she wants. This is helpful to the person shopping with her, because it means we don't have to spend hours upon hours in the store. Peyton started handing me things to hold. I made comments like "I like your choice," or "That will go great with your brown skirt," or "Do you need anything to wear with that?"

I felt a bit nostalgic as I remembered my own upbringing. I always appreciated the freedom my mother gave me in picking out my own clothes, even though I had to live with the consequences if I bought one expensive thing versus several medium priced things. I'm sure she had to bite her lip many times as I showed off my latest "deal."

Fortunately for me, Peyton is still at the age where she is just as happy with sturdy staple clothes from the discount store as she is with a few really cute things from more expensive pre-teen stores. We shop at both.

On this shopping trip, we "Oohed" and "Ahhed" together as she tried on various things. We have a mutual understanding that you shouldn't buy something unless you absolutely *love* it and it looks really good on you. That avoids getting it home and never wearing it again.

This time, she happened to love *everything* she brought into the fitting room. She tried on some things twice, just to double check. Then it came time to tally it all up.

> PW: I want it all.
>
> SW: I'm sure you do – they're all cute, but our budget today is $200. Let's see what it adds up to.

We then used this as a mathematical exercise. The total came to roughly $265.

> SW: Okay, which things are we going to take out?
>
> PW: But I want it all. (Grimacing.)

That's when I knew we would be spending more time in the store to work on the issue of gratitude.

> SW: Peyton, we have $200 to spend today. I have more money than that, but that's what our budget is. So, what pieces do you want to get today?

We looked at the various combinations of how we could get to $200, and she chose the items that fit into the budget. Still, disappointment was all over her face.

> SW: I can see you're disappointed, but $200 is a lot of money to spend on clothes. I'll tell you what; I'll take these beautiful clothes you picked out, and I'll walk around the store with them. When you're satisfied that these are what you want, then come and let me know and we'll get them.

Her head was low as she and I walked out of the dressing room. There have been days when we have gone into a store and right away have gotten things she loved, but this wasn't that day, and the lesson for this trip was clear.

I walked around the store, clothes in hand, for around five minutes, when Peyton came up to me and said in a soft, sad voice:

PW: I'm ready.

SW: Why don't you take a little more time, and when you

can come back and be really glad to be getting all

these clothes, then we'll buy them.

She walked away and I continued looking around. Another ten minutes passed and again, with a soft voice and sad face (but a little more energy) she said:

PW: I'm ready to buy the clothes.

SW: I hear you, but when you can come back and be

really glad to be getting these clothes, then we'll buy

them.

She rolled her eyes at me and walked away. I knew I was onto something. I was battling the kids' television shows where girls live lavish lifestyles and spend endless amounts of money; getting things from a sense of entitlement. This was what I was up against, and I knew this wasn't who she was, so I held my ground without judgment against her.

A whole ten minutes later, she came up to me, with a different attitude.

PW: Mom, thank you for the clothes. I'm ready.

SW: Great! Let's go buy them. You've made some great

choices.

Moral of the story: she's loved and worn every piece of clothing we bought that day with pride. She also respects our budget, and says "thank you" now whenever we go shopping for clothes.

Peyton's Point of View

I'm grateful for my dog, my cat, my mom, my dad, my house, my church, my marshmallow shooter, my plants, my clothes, my features, the fact that I can walk. It makes me feel good to think about those things. But if I didn't have those things I could still be grateful because I am alive.

Questions for Reflection:
1. What are five things for which you are grateful today? Take time for both of you to answer (and you can't use the same one twice.)
2. Were you surprised at anything the other person said?
3. The next time, try adding one more, and the next time, another. You might want to keep track of your lists in a notebook each day and review it together over time. You'll be amazed at how this exercise can turn attitudes around.
4. What is something about yourself for which you are grateful?
5. Can you collect up to 200 things on your list?

Glass Half Empty or Half Full?

I am an optimist at heart. I tend to see the possibilities in situations, at least most of the time. The question "Is the glass half empty or half full?" was a fun concept to introduce to my daughter. Like any child (or adult), she would complain about this or that on any given day. One day, instead of criticizing her for whining, I said, "It sounds like you're seeing the glass half empty." This immediately intrigued her. She not only wanted to know what I meant but also why I hadn't fallen into my normal corrective of, "Stop whining!" We started what has become a game between us but also has the bonus of teaching logic and reasoning. For instance, here is a conversation we had recently:

> SW: You've got ten thank-you notes to write after your birthday party.
>
> PW: Do I really *have* to?
>
> SW: Now, what would be the 'Glass half empty' response?
>
> PW: (In a tired monotone) I've got ten notes to write.
>
> SW: Now what is the 'glass half full' response?
>
> PW: (Pause for thinking.) I've got ten notes to write, and I can take my time writing them.
>
> SW: That's one way to look at it. What's another idea?
>
> PW: Wow, I got ten gifts at my party that I can say thank you for!

After that, she caught on to the concept so well, that when I complain about something, she'll quip, "Mom, glass half full!"

Ugh ... busted.

Peyton's Point of View
The glass half full is saying something good about something and the glass half empty is complaining about it. Sometimes there's not a good side to something and you need to complain. Sometimes you just need to talk about it.

Questions for Reflection:
1. What's something you dread doing?
2. What would the "glass half empty" response be?
3. What would the "glass half full" response be?
4. What are some reasons to use the glass half full approach in your family?
5. When are some instances where you would want to choose the glass half empty response?

Lying and Telling the Truth

This is a tough one. All children and adults tell lies at some point in their lives. I admit, when I smell a lie, it's hard for me to let it go. As a child, I never dreamed of telling my parents an outright lie, for fear of the consequences that would follow. That certainly doesn't mean, however, that I didn't deflect blame onto others and commit sins of "omission."

One day my daughter kept a lie going for a good thirty minutes about having already done her nightly reading for school. After an initial conversation, I was not convinced she was telling me the truth. I asked her several times if she was telling me the truth and she coolly said "Yes." Still not satisfied, I came back again from a different angle: "Tell me what your chapter was about in the story tonight." She came up with something quicker than I thought possible. Finally after several rounds of this, she "fessed" up.

Here I fell into fear. I was horrified that she had lied to me. After issuing some consequences, we were fine again, but I was left in bewilderment and fear. I thought, "Oh my God, if it's starting now, what will it be like when she's a teenager? What will she try to hide from me then? She's smart and convincing, oh my God, *I don't have control over her anymore!*"

Once I recognized my underlying fear, I realized I never had control over her anyway. It is true, I can't control if she chooses to tell me the truth. But I wasn't creating an environment where she felt free to make a mistake without me coming down on her.

If we want to teach our children to be the best people they can be, we've got to be on the beam ourselves – all the time. Or else be really good at admitting it when we fall off that elusive beam.

Children are smart. It's hard to encourage them to tell the truth when they see so many stories on the news of our elected officials being arrested for yet another corruption scandal. Perhaps those instances are opportunities to have more conversations.

Whether one makes a habit of telling the truth or lying on a regular basis directly relates to integrity. Many people have defined integrity as how a person acts when no one else is looking. To be able to "do the right thing" in spite of any outer reinforcement requires immense inner strength, a clear ability to know right from wrong, and the ability to tell oneself and others the truth. Children need their parents and other adult role models to show them that "doing the right thing" no matter what the cost, and no matter who is watching, is important. Living a life of integrity means your inner sense of truth matches your outer actions.

Peyton and I once overheard a conversation in the airport waiting area. A twenty-something young man and his father were sitting near us, when the airline crew announced that they had oversold the flight. They needed volunteers to surrender their tickets. The promise of $400 in flight and meal vouchers was enticing to the son who saw a way to take advantage of the situation, if his father would lie. Evidently his younger brother was a "no show." The older son told his father he should check the younger son in anyway, saying he was down the hall, thereby getting the voucher. The father said, "Good idea," and went to ask about it, but was told the younger son needed to be there in person to refuse the ticket. The conversation continued with the son trying to figure out how they could get around the system and get the vouchers.

At that point I turned to Peyton, who was listening to all of this and said:

> SW: He was not setting a good example of telling the
> truth, was he?

She knew exactly what was going on, and she was waiting for me to say something about it. Fortunately, at that moment, I was conscious.

> SW: What should he have done?
>
> PW: The son shouldn't have said that to the dad and the
> dad shouldn't have agreed.

She was exactly right.

Is there ever a time when telling a lie is appropriate? What about Santa, or a surprise party? What if the truth will hurt someone's feelings? How do you reconcile those situations as a parent? I believe there is a way to tell the truth in a kind and generous way. If someone gives you something that you can't stand, you can still respond with love and graciousness for the thought behind the gift. It takes some extra thinking, but the idea is to be truthful in big things as well as in small things.

Peyton's Point of View

Telling the truth is better than lying because you can get in way more trouble if you lie. Just tell the truth in the beginning. When someone lies to me, I don't feel good. It hurts my feelings. I feel left out like there's a secret or something. It makes me think they don't want to be friends anymore and just want to keep secrets.

Questions for Reflection (for parents):
1. Do you lie? Does your child lie?
2. Has your child ever witnessed you lying?
3. Is lying acceptable to you, as a parent?
4. How do you respond when you discover your child is lying?
5. Have you ever talked with your child about a lie you've told?
6. Does your child lie often?

7. Do you do the right thing when no one else is looking?
8. Is it important to you for your child to have integrity?
9. How do you communicate that value to your child?

Questions for Reflection (for parents and children):
1. How does it feel when you lie to anyone?
2. Why do you think people lie?
3. Why do you lie?
4. How can I help you so you don't feel that you need to lie to me?
5. Do you understand that we don't lie in this household?
6. Is there anything you need to tell me right now?
7. Do you see me doing the right thing all the time? When?
8. How do you feel about that?

Loss

When Peyton's father and I separated, we needed to move from our house. This meant she would have to go to a different elementary school. I dreaded having to tell her this and started thinking about how I might approach it.

One day soon afterwards, she said to me out of the blue, "Mom, I sure wish I could go to the other school in town." My ears perked up – was I dreaming? "Why do you say that?" I asked. "Well, I really like my friends from summer day camp and they all go to the other school."

Secretly shouting a big "thank you" inside, I said, "Well, let's see what we can do about that," not wanting to sound too eager. I asked her what friends she would miss from her current school and she named a few. I assured her that we could continue to have play dates with them and that in a few years she would be back in school with them in the local Middle School.

Who knows how much she really "got" in that conversation? When it came time to actually put the plan into action, there was some back peddling, as I imagined there would be.

The loss of the family life we shared was felt over the next years in a variety of ways. I'm a firm believer in being as straightforward as possible, while being age-appropriate. I never spoke badly about her father, but also did not leave issues so shrouded in mystery that she would wonder if we would get back together. Most children of divorce want their parents to get back together. I had to be clear with Peyton, when she would "fish" around, that this would not happen.

After many months, we sold our old house where we had lived as a family. The night before we turned it over to the new owners, we went to say a final good-bye. I burst into tears when we walked inside the doors. All the stress of the previous eight months it had been on the market poured out. Confronted with the fact that this part of our lives was over, there was another door of grief I had yet to walk through. As soon as she saw me crying, it gave Peyton permission to cry too. It wasn't a long uncontrollable cry. It was just enough for us to know that something significant was happening. A chapter in our lives was closing.

We created our own ritual by going into each room and reminisced, thanking the room for the time we had enjoyed there. We did the same thing outside. By the time we were finished, we were ready to go, and we drove away feeling a bit more whole.

Losses can come in many forms. Perhaps you've lost a relative, friend, or a pet. Adults may not realize the significance these losses can be for a child, but they are real and need to be dealt with. Sometimes a child (or an adult, for that matter) may think that opening the door into feelings of loss may be too overwhelming, so he pushes them away. We say kids are resilient, but everything reshapes our hearts.

We all remember losses from our childhoods, don't we? Rituals are often helpful and provide an opportunity to share feelings. Not talking about a loss can cause severe damage to children both in the short and the long term. If the adult cannot talk about her feelings in an appropriate manner in front of her children, they may feel isolated, and leave their feelings unresolved.

Different faith traditions provide rituals to help people deal with the biggest loss, death. In Judaism, for example, friends and family participate in "sitting Shiva," which is a week-long period of grief following the death of an immediate family member. People visit, bring food, and provide comfort to those who have lost a loved one.

In Japan, where Shinto Buddhism is the predominant religion, an altar is made in the home of the person who has died, adorned with pictures, candles and offerings of the person's favorite foods. They believe that a person's spirit may stay around to complete unfinished business for up to 49 days. The items on the altar honor the deceased and recognize needs for food while his spirit is still present. They also believe the spirits of the dead return each year to check on things before leaving again. These customs can be helpful in the grieving process.

Wakes in the Christian tradition are used mostly in the Roman Catholic Church. The purpose is to allow mourners the opportunity to recognize the finality of death and to say good-bye. Protestants, for the most part, don't have wakes. They believe the spirit of the deceased immediately goes to be with God. While there is an opportunity to mourn and grieve, the focus shifts to celebrating the life of the person, rather than the death.

Peyton's Point of View
It doesn't feel good to lose something. You feel like you have a black hole or something in your stomach because it's gone and you don't know what to do. It can hurt your heart. You may show it to

others by being mean or start being mad and then you start crying, because it's not easy to talk about it. But having others support you while you're talking about it helps. What would I say to someone who lost someone they loved? I'd say, "You always know they loved you and they probably wished for you a really good life. You can know they'll be thinking of you, just like God does."

Questions for Reflection:
1. Have you ever felt sad over something or someone you've lost? (For example, a pet, parent, friend, grandparent, house, or feeling of safety.)
2. How have you dealt with your feelings about it?
3. Did you have some kind of ritual to mark the event?
4. If you haven't talked about this loss, why do you think you haven't?
5. What is one memory you have about that person, place or thing you've lost?
6. Can you talk about why the person, place, or thing was important to you?
7. If it's too hard to think about it, can you write about it in a private journal?
8. What is a way you can keep the memory alive?
9. Is there anything we need to talk about right now?

Note: If you need more resources to help deal with grief and loss, check with your clergy, local grieving centers, local mental health services, or a therapist. There are also summer camps for grieving children to be with peers in similar situations. (See Resource section.)

Spirituality: Go Inside and Listen

Spirituality can be defined as "connecting with God, others and yourself." Many people these days consider themselves more "spiritual" than "religious," although many adults tend to reconnect back to the religion of their youth when their children are little.

Life events such as First Communion, Baptism, Confirmation, Bar or Bat Mitzvah can pull adults who walked away from their faith tradition for a while back to their religious roots. Some discover they want their children to have the religious training and traditions they did. Others, however, have painful memories of their faith traditions from childhood and do not choose to return to avoid putting their children through what they experienced.

Children are spiritual by nature and will ask questions about their role in the universe and how it all fits together. Encouraging their sense of spirituality helps them to connect with something greater than themselves and can foster hope, faith and even a sense of optimism.

I have had conversations with many parents over the years who regretted not having given their children any kind of spiritual upbringing, based on their own negative experiences. Racked with guilt, some remain frozen, not making any decision about what to do. When something happens, there's no community or structure in place to support them.

So how do you talk about the mysterious topic of spirituality? In the early part of the twentieth century, French philosopher Pierre Theilhard de Chardin wrote, "We're not human beings having a spiritual experience, we're spiritual beings having a human experience." In other words, our very beings are spiritual. Therefore, everything we do is in some way spiritual. It's just a matter of seeing it that way.

"I'm bored" is one of my favorite expressions. Fortunately I haven't fallen into the trap of trying to figure out something for my daughter to do when she makes this statement to me.

"Hmm," I say. "I always heard that being bored means you're not using your imagination enough. How could you make this moment really fun for yourself?" Or, "What are some things you have been wanting to do for a while, but have not had the opportunity to get to? Maybe there is an unopened toy from a birthday party, or a book that is waiting to be read." I try to avoid suggesting the television.

"I'm bored" may also signal something deeper.

One afternoon I decided to try something that I had just heard at a seminar on "Spiritual Parenting," taught by Susan Fisher, which was based on the work of Dr. Thomas Hora. This exercise takes some time to practice but it's worth every minute because it helps child to listen and begin to trust their inner voice.

Peyton was very fidgety in the back seat. I knew she was tired, but I also felt there was something else going on, so I used a tool from the seminar: the question "What is God's good idea for you right now?" Here's how it went:

> SW: You're acting in a way that is different for you. Do you know what is going on for you right now?
>
> PW: No, I'm bored.
>
> SW: Hmm …what is God's good idea for you right now?
>
> PW: I don't know. (Looking at me oddly.)
>
> SW: God has a good idea just waiting for you right now, see if you can go inside to understand what it is that you need to do.

We waited, Peyton in the back seat and me in the driver's seat. After about four or five minutes, I asked:

> SW: What did you learn when you went inside?
>
> PW: Nothing! (Disgusted.) I don't hear anything.
>
> SW: Go back inside. I just know that there is some idea for you.

Again we waited for what seemed to be an eternity, but it was probably only another three or four minutes.

PW: Ugh, I don't hear anything.

SW: Try again. Remember, God has a good idea about what's going on. What is it? I'm going to walk inside for a minute to take these groceries in, but I want you to stay here and see what you hear. This is really important.

I came back out in a minute or two and sat down in the back seat with her.

Silence.

SW: If you go inside you can really know what you are feeling. Do you have a sense that you're being told what to do from the inside? That your heart knows what to do?

Silence.

SW: Your heart knows which way to go and knows how to make a good decision or a bad decision – to goof off or not goof off.

PW: Does it take time to learn how to do?

SW: Yeah…but it's worth it.

More Silence.

PW: I'm lonely … that's what I'm feeling. (She started to cry.)

We hugged and I told her I loved her.

Wow. I wish I had been as in touch with myself when I was her age. She got it.

The proof she got it on some level came about a year later. Peyton had a play date over and was acting kind of wild. From what I observed, she was trying to impress her girlfriend. We have a code phrase for when she is "not in her body," meaning that she isn't grounded and is not acting out of a place centered in self-esteem.

I pulled her aside and asked her:

> SW: Hey, what's up? You're acting like you're out of your
> body – kind of over the top.

She stopped to think for a minute and then she went back to playing. Later, after her friend went home, we talked about it.

> SW: What was going on for you this afternoon? You
> seemed a little out of sorts.

Peyton thought again and then confidently said:

> PW: I was feeling a little insecure and I wanted some
> attention, so I started making jokes and acting crazy.

I congratulated her on knowing herself so well. Wow.
I went on to say:

> SW: Your behavior concerned me because when I see
> people acting that way, trying to impress other
> people and doing crazy things to make them laugh,
> it tells me you're uncomfortable in your skin.
> Sometimes people who feel that way do things to
> please others and hurt themselves, and I don't want
> that for you.

She listened and as we hugged I told her I loved her.

Peyton's Point of View

I hate this, it's boring and hard. But if you go inside your body, and you feel it and you say, "Am I really acting this way," and "Is this how I'm feeling," sometimes it could be good. For example if you're really nervous about something before something really important, you can go inside your body and calm yourself down.

Questions for Spirituality: Go Inside and Listen
1. What do you feel like when everything is quiet?
2. What kinds of thoughts go through your head when you are alone?

3. Do you feel connected to your inner thoughts and feelings? If so, how do show that connection?
4. Do you feel connected with other people? How do you show that connection?
5. If you were without adult supervision for a period of time, how confident are you that you would be OK?

Talking About God

Obviously, as an ordained Christian minister, I speak out of my experience. However, I have worked extensively with other faith groups. Please feel free to substitute any name for the Holy which feels comfortable to you and your tradition. I have included some examples of practices from Judaism, Buddhism, and Islam along with different ideas within the Christian tradition. The saying, "Take what you want and leave the rest" certainly applies here.

Children know about God. They just do. Whether they hear about God directly or indirectly, they have some idea about the Creator of the Universe, the Holy of Holies, Higher Power, or however you refer to God. But just what are children internalizing at a young age and what shapes their theology, or ideas about God?

During the years I've led Confirmation Classes (eighth grade), I have been moved to conduct my own research on the topic. As we begin to study about God, I ask the kids to draw the first image they remember ever having about God. Hands down, almost every student (and most of them have been Caucasian) has drawn an old white man with a long white beard sitting high up on a cloud in "Heaven."

That's also the conception I had growing up about what God looked like. I knew that God loved me, but I also modeled "Him" after my earthly father. So, while I knew He loved me, I also was very afraid of doing anything that would get Him angry for fear of what punishment might lie ahead.

Having come a long way from where I began in my theology, I knew my daughter must feel differently. So I decided to have a conversation with her to see what she thought.

SW: Do you have an idea about what God looks like?

PW: He has a beard.

SW: So God's a man who has a beard?

PW: Yes. An old man with a beard.

SW: Where did you see that?

PW: I don't know.

SW: If you were standing in front of God right now, what would you ask him?

PW: How did you make earth?

SW: What's his personality like?

PW: He's usually happy. But if it storms, it's because he's mad and we did the wrong thing.

SW: Really? Wow. So, he kind of bites back with a storm?

PW: Yeah. Sometimes if it's lightening, he's furious.

SW: What's he angry at?

PW: Maybe somebody did the wrong thing like a robber robbed a bank.

SW: So, if you do something bad, does God get mad at you?

PW: It has to be really bad.

SW: Can people be forgiven for doing bad things?

PW: Yeah. Like in the Lord's Prayer it says, "Forgive us our trespasses and we forgive those who trespass against us."

SW: And what does that mean?

PW: That if someone does something wrong you can

forgive him while we are being forgiven.

SW: Have you ever done anything you need to be forgiven for?

PW: Privacy … please!

SW: When you do something bad, how does that make
you feel?

PW: You feel bad. You feel that you shouldn't have done it.

Peyton's perception of God as a vengeful old man came without my ever having said anything remotely close to that. I have never referred to God as even male and certainly not an angry one. Somehow she picked up this idea within our culture. Maybe she remembers a painting in a museum. Maybe I haven't done enough to teach her about some of the many images of God which are in the scriptures, both male (shepherd, Father, Prince of Peace) and female (mother breast-feeding her child, woman looking for a lost coin), animal (mother eagle, hen) and beyond human (I am, that I am), and force of nature (pillar of fire, wind).

A friend from seminary, an African-American pastor, says her conversations with children aren't about what God looks like. Instead she says they talk about what difference God makes in their lives and how they can live their lives in a better way as a result of knowing God.

HERE ARE SOME OF THE THINGS ABOUT GOD I WANT MY DAUGHTER TO KNOW:

- You are made in the image of God

- God loves you, no matter what

- God forgives you, no matter what

- God's love frees you to love yourself and others

- You are never alone

The idea that God loves you right now, just as you are, goes against many of the cultural messages in Western society. Battered by low self esteem, many people have ideas of God as a sort of good and bad Santa. If you are good, God gives you stuff, and if you are bad, God takes it away and punishes you. The idea that God loves you, unconditionally, just because you are a human being, is profound. No amount of effort on our parts will make God love one person above another. That's called grace and it is the great equalizer of all humanity.

Many parents suffer from "theological whippings" in their childhood. They were told by religious authorities that they were "bad" for being human in one way or another. That belief can translate to how we love our kids. Our ability to receive unconditional love and acceptance from God directly correlates to our ability to give and receive unconditional love and acceptance from others, including our children.

In seminary, I learned that as our self-esteem increases and changes over time, if our images of God don't also change, over time we grow away from our ability to tap into our spiritual resources. So, as we mature emotionally and psychologically, our spiritual lives need to mature also or else we may find ourselves abandoning our faith and we won't be able to guide our children in their own spiritual growth.

That's what happened for me. It took me many years to break out of what I now consider a narrow sense of God and set of beliefs that I developed as a child. Over time, I came to realize my faith was based in fear. As I did, I knew I must change. I felt terrified that my world as I had always known it would fall apart. I realized I didn't know what I believed without other people telling me. And what was worse, because I had always been theologically spoon-fed, I didn't know how to grow spiritually on my own. I began a careful process of deconstructing the negative theology onto which I had clung so desperately, and reconstructing a theology which fit my experience of a living, loving and liberating God as known through the scriptures. That process allowed me to maintain a sense of vibrant faith which continues to grow and evolve.

I had the opportunity to take Peyton with me to several different houses of worship in her early years. We've been to services in Synagogues, Mosques, and a variety of different types of Christian communities. I want her to know that there are many ways people communicate with God and that I welcome her exploration, while I am exposing her to our tradition every Sunday in church.

As your children grow up, they will ask you what you think about God, and even if you don't answer, your actions or inaction will tell them. If you don't want to pass on what you learned as a child, start exploring what you believe together. If a religious institution such as a Church, Synagogue, Mosque or Temple isn't your thing, try reading books. For example, *Old Turtle* is a wonderful children's book which portrays God as an old female turtle. Or talk together about how you see the work of creation in art or nature.

Questions for Reflection (for parents):

> *For some, this may be a difficult exercise to complete, but I encourage you to spend some time thinking about your answers. All our thoughts gained through acceptance or in reaction to those things we learned, stay with us until we actually change them. So you may reject the idea of the angry God you had as a child, but until you actually change that idea into another image in your consciousness, that idea will remain within you, even if you're only reacting to it.*
>
> *Our children aren't born with the baggage we have. Help them explore in their own way, so they can avoid "unpacking the bags" later on in life.*

1. What did you learn about the nature of God as a child, if anything? Was your God loving, or vengeful? Kind and compassionate or mean and judgmental? Do you still believe in that God?
2. What did you learn about how God interacts with human-kind? Was God distant, or very personal? Did God punish or forgive freely? Did your God bring tragedy on humans in the form of natural disaster or illness? Do you still believe that?
3. What did you learn about the afterlife when you were young? Do you still believe that?
4. What were you taught about Satan or the devil, if anything? Do you still believe that?
5. What were you taught about the role of the community of faith when you were a child? Do you still believe that?
6. What were you taught about other faiths when you were a child? Do you still believe that?
7. What did you experience from the clergy in your life? Were they believable and trustworthy?
8. Were you able to maintain a sense of faith in elementary school, middle school and high school?
9. Were there any major events in your life that either made you gain or lose faith?
10. Have you ever been angry at God? Did you resolve it or do you still hold it?
11. If you weren't raised with a concept of God, do you still agree with that or would you do it differently now?

Questions for Reflection (parents and children):
1. If you could draw a picture of God, what would God look like?
2. Have you ever experienced God in your life?
3. What do you think our role as humans is here on the earth in relation to God?
4. When you look out into a starry night, or around you in

the woods, do you feel close to God? Do you wonder how it all came to be?

5. Do you think there are other beings, such as angels, which help us?

6. If God could say something to you that you could hear, what do you think it would be?

Why Do Bad Things Happen?

One Sunday morning I invited the children in the church where I served to ask any question they had and I would try to answer it. "Why do bad things happen?" was one that several of them asked. I imagine it was a question on the minds of the adults sitting in the pews, too!

Everyone knows someone who has experienced something bad in their lives. Perhaps a family member or pet has died, or parents have divorced, or natural disasters have hit areas of the world, leaving many hurt or dead, such as Hurricane Katrina. Parents often feel helpless in knowing how to answer their children. Sometimes it's because we don't want to see our children suffer. Sometimes it's because we feel uncomfortable with loss ourselves.

Here's what I said to the children that morning in church: "The reality is, we don't know why certain things happen. They just do in a world where human beings are in charge. Sometimes human beings have failed in their responsibility to do what they can to help. Good things and bad things happen in our world. The important thing to know is, that we are not alone. We have each other. God is with us. God does not control what happens to us in the world like a person controls a puppet, but God is there to comfort us when we are hurting. God cries with us when we cry. We are never alone."

One of the skills I learned when I served as a hospital chaplain was the importance of being pastorally present with someone who is in distress. The ability of being a "non-anxious presence in an anxious environment" is one of the greatest gifts you can give to anyone. It can be hard to do in certain situations, but it is done simply by offering a supportive, silent presence. As I sat with people who had heard bad news, I quickly learned that they didn't need words to explain "why" something was happening, and they didn't need to hear religious platitudes from me. (The all time worst is saying to someone after their child has died, "God must have needed another little angel in heaven.") If I felt compelled to offer some kind of explanation, I discovered it was usually to make *me* feel better. I also discovered people in distress don't need another person drawn into the emotions of the situation. Rather, they need someone who is calm and able to hear their feelings. Most often, they just need to know they are not alone and that someone is there supporting them in prayerful silence, caring for them in the depth of the pain they are facing. Sometimes a few words are appropriate but mostly power comes in sitting there engaged and in silence.

Our children can benefit greatly from periods of supportive silence from us, sprinkled with a few well-chosen words. Don't get me wrong, your child needs to know you are there, but giving space for mystery and for feelings is a treasured gift you can give to people of all ages.

At an appropriate time, you can try some reflective listening to help put words on feelings in a situation which might be confusing. For example, a conversation after learning of the death of a pet, for example, may go something like this:

Child: (crying)

Parent: (Hug) It's so sad.

Child: Why, Mom, why did he die?

Parent: You have deep questions …

Child: Yeah, it's not fair … he didn't do anything wrong.
Why did he have to die?

Parent: You want answers. You're feeling helpless.

Child: (crying) I miss him so much. How will I go to
sleep tonight without him?

Parent: (silence) I know you miss him. There's a hole
inside and it's lonely.

Child: (crying) I'm so sad.

Parent: (silence, hugging) I know, honey.

By reflecting back your child's feelings, the conversation is about her, not about you. Her job right then is to work through what's going on in her own mind, not to take care of you, the parent. If you respond with your own feelings and thoughts (which may or may not be appropriate to share later on down the road) you can derail her need to process grief. You may not get another opportunity, if she doesn't feel heard.

Peyton's Point of View
You think that bad things happen sometimes, but they really turn out not to be all that bad. You always know that God is with you and you're always being loved, even if you do something bad.

Questions for Reflection (at a time when nothing difficult is happening):
1. How would you answer the question "Why do bad things happen?"
2. How would your child answer that question?
3. What do you think you would do if something bad happened to you?
4. What would help you the most?
5. Can you remember a time when you were able to be present and a "non-anxious presence" to someone?
6. What specifically did you do/not do?

Questions for Reflection (after something happens – use after initial processing of feelings):

1. What makes you sad/angry/helpless (or any other feeling) about this situation?
2. Do you know what you need right now? (It's okay if your child doesn't know right then; it gets them thinking about it.)
3. How can I help you get what you need right now? Later?

Prayer and Meditation

Prayer

People of most every faith group pray. People without a faith tradition also pray. In Judaism, Christianity and Islam, followers pray to the same God, although by different names. People talk with God and listen to God, plead with God, and rant to God. God doesn't care how it sounds or if we make sense. In fact, God knows what's in our hearts already. God is always there to hear you no matter what time of the day or night it is. God cares about everything you have to say. If you feel bad about something that happened in your day, or if you've done something wrong, you can tell God and God will listen. You can always ask for forgiveness for anything you feel may have created distance between you and God and God will *always* make the relationship right again if you are sincere.

Prayer requires the use of imagination. In the New Testament the apostle Paul says, "Now faith is the assurance of things hoped for, the conviction of things not seen." Ancient church mystics used their imaginations regularly as they spoke of visions given to them by God. The Scriptures are full of stories of miracles that encourage us to see beyond what is seen. In Judaism, stories are told and retold of their history as a people following God. For people to imagine what their ancestors went through, it requires the use of imagination. The Torah as well as Rabbinical literature is full of stories rich in imagery that recall the events of the history of a people who have experienced trials and triumphs of faith: the Covenant made with Abraham and Sarah, the bondage of the Hebrew people, the Exodus and the search for the land flowing with milk and honey, and the countless remembrances of a faithful God amid the daily flow of life all pull on the imagination of the faithful. Rituals of many faiths, such as the Passover Seder, Baptism, Purim, The Hajj, the Eucharist/Mass/Holy Communion, and even funerals, ask the participant to draw upon some form of imagination to connect them with their experience of the Holy. Rituals may also connect us with those present as well as ancient communities who have observed the same practices. That connection requires us to imagine their presence with us.

Prayer *isn't* about asking God for things like you would ask of Santa! God is not in the business of getting big or small toys, making people act a certain way or having things go your way. Here's a conversation that came up for us one day.

> PW: Mom, pray for me that I'll win this game! (She yelled as she madly worked the buttons on the Nintendo DS game.)
>
> SW: What?
>
> PW: Quick, I'm almost at level seven and I want to win.
>
> SW: (Big dilemma.) I can't pray for *that* – how about I pray that you do your very best?
>
> She won. Then I had to explain why:
>
> SW: Praying for a certain outcome on a DS game is tricky, because if you lose, does that mean God doesn't want you to win at DS? I don't think it matters to God if you win at DS right now or not, but doing your best

and feeling good about yourself is certainly something God cares about.

I'm reminded of a game the Yankees were playing when Joe Torre was still manager. It made the news that Joe's sister had prayed the Yankees would win. That kind of puts God in a pickle, doesn't it? Suppose someone from the other team had a relative praying to God that *they* would win. Whose side would God be on? What if the other side had a priest praying? How about a rabbi? Then you could have a real controversy going! Whose prayer trumps whose?

The point is, God is involved and interested in us; the Psalms even say the very number of hairs on our heads is known, but does God care who wins a Nintendo DS game or even a Yankees game?

In the bigger scheme of things, I talked with Peyton about the role of God's will in prayer. "When we say The Lord's Prayer, we say, 'Thy Kingdom come, Thy Will be done,'" I began. "What does that mean? It means that we are asking God to answer prayer the way God sees fit in the larger scheme of things. We don't know if asking for a certain thing is ultimately in the best interest of everything or everybody involved. By praying for God's will to be done, we are saying that we trust that God knows what's best. Certainly we can ask for specific things in our prayers, but we trust that God will do with them what God wills."

This was all a bit much, in relation to the Nintendo DS game, but it was a good time to open the issue for a future time.

What are some questions you want to ask God? Parents need not be worried if they don't know how to answer them. You can always investigate together how you think God may answer a particular prayer based on how you read your sacred texts or talk with a faith leader in your tradition. The important thing is being free enough to ask the questions. I believe God welcomes all of our questions and even our doubts. God is big enough to handle it all.

As a minister, I have spent some time in Church School classes talking about prayer with elementary school-aged children and have been profoundly touched by the level of their prayers. They have asked for prayers for pets who are ill, for families in their communities who have had a relative get sick or die. They have prayed for other communities they have heard about in the news, or people affected by natural disasters. They have asked for prayers during breakups of families, for parents who are in distress. You name it, they've thought about it and felt that prayer might help. When and how do you pray? Prayer can be done anywhere and at anytime. You can pray at home, in bed, at meals, on the school bus, out on the playground, in worship at your church, synagogue, mosque, or temple. You can pray whenever you need guidance. The important thing to communicate is that God is always there for you, listening to you, however you come to God. You don't need a special formula. There is no magic to it.

Prayer is a conversation, and the more you do it, the more comfortable you will feel.

At the beginning, you may want to model prayer for your children. While children are very free in their prayers, they oftentimes want to hear what their parents pray for also. If you feel self conscious, tell them. You can pray together, if you want. Explore it together!

These are some prayers which have been around for a long time. Remember this one?

> *Now I lay me down to sleep.*
>
> *I pray the Lord my soul to keep.*

If I should die before I wake,

I pray the Lord my soul to take.

It's no wonder we got any sleep at all while we wondered if the good Lord would snatch us away while we slept!

Prayers at meals:

God is great, God is good, let us thank Him for our food. Amen!

Then everyone digs in … short, sweet and covers the basics.

Moravian Prayer:

Come, Lord Jesus, our guest to be and bless these gifts bestowed by Thee.

Bless our loved ones everywhere and keep them in thy loving care. Amen.

This is also short and to the point, but a bit fancy in the language. I always wondered if God spoke with all those "thees" and "thous!"

Prayer from the Jewish Tradition; used for the first night of every holiday:

Thank you for giving us life.

Thank you for sustaining us in life.

Thank you for bringing us to this moment.

Rabbi Vicki Axe says, "By intoning these words we are saying, I am alive! I am aware! I see the world around me! I see the people around me. I see blessings in the littlest things. I feel God's presence all around me and inside of me."

What elements do you include in your prayers? I once learned this simple formula: Adoration, Thanksgiving, Supplication, and Conclusion.

> **Adoration**: Start by addressing God with things you know about who God is, such as God of all creation, God who loves each of us, God who comes to us like a Father or Mother.
>
> **Thanksgiving**: Thank God for things for which you are grateful – a good day, family, a bed to sleep in, health, love, etc.
>
> **Supplication**: This is where you tell God your concerns and make requests.
>
> **Conclusion**: You can end your requests, thanking God again for having heard you and close with Amen, which simply means: May it be so!

Peyton's Point of View

If you're sad, you can ask God for love and help. If someone's hurt you can ask God to help her to get better. God is close to me ... I feel it.

Questions for Reflection (for parents):

1. What was your practice of praying when you were a child?
2. Did you ever have a sense that God was listening to you?
3. If your experience of communicating with God was distant, is there anything you can do to change that?
4. How comfortable are you praying in front of someone else?
5. Do you think God is there and listening to you now?
6. What is your perspective on the purpose of your prayer?
7. Has God ever answered your prayers with a "no?"
8. Have you ever felt that God has answered your prayers positively?
9. If yes, can you describe that to your child?

10. What are the things for which you are grateful that you can include regularly in your prayers?

Questions for Reflection (for parents and children):
1. When you pray, to whom to do you pray?
2. Do you think anyone is listening?
3. What kind of things do you ask for in your prayers?
4. Have your prayers been answered?
5. Is there anything you would be afraid to pray for? What is it? And why?
6. If you could sit down with God and ask God anything in the world, what would it be?

Meditation

The ability to be at home and at peace in one's own body is a skill which many adults do not have. If we can teach our children to feel comfortable inside themselves, they will benefit immensely. One of the ways to get to that place is through the use of meditation and guided imagery.

Guided imagery is a useful tool that helps us transcend our current situations and believe in something more. For many years I have practiced meditation as taught by Jesuit and Buddhist practitioners. Not only has my spiritual life and faith deepened as a result, but my awareness of myself in the world has increased too. Many of us think that children are too young to participate, but the fact is, meditation and simple exercises of guided imagery can help relax, clear the mind, and strengthen people of any age. Let me illustrate with a few exercises:

A. A MEDITATION FOR RELAXATION AND OPENNESS (APPROPRIATE FOR ALL AGES):

Find a quiet place to sit still and relax uninterrupted for a few minutes. You can sit or lie down and keep your eyes open or closed. Read the following slowly and softly to your child.

Begin to breathe … notice your breath coming in, and then flowing out. In and then out. Slowly, let it go deeper and deeper. Each time you breathe in, follow your breath in through your nose, down the back of your throat, down through your windpipe, into your lungs, filling your lungs all the way until they are full. The next time you breathe in, hold your breath there for five seconds and then breathe out slowly ... let it out all the way until there is no more breath in you. During the next breath, count slowly six beats, following your breath all the way down. Hold it for three seconds and then slowly release your breath over six beats. Continue to breathe in and out slowly, relaxing and releasing. And then, when you are ready, slowly open your eyes.

Here's another variation: practice breathing in, saying silently: "I breathe in love, peace and forgiveness," and upon exhaling, "I let go of fear, stress and anger." (When breathing in you can substitute any positive words such as God, light, life, goodness, gratitude, mercy, abundance etc., and when breathing out substitute fear, anger, confusion, jealousy, etc.)

Repeat this over and over and you'll be amazed at how quickly your body relaxes, your attitude changes and your mind opens up to new possibilities. This type of exercise is not new. Practices like these have been in existence for millennia.

Here are some exercises for those who are more visual:

B. FINDING AN INNER SACRED PLACE (AGES SIX AND UP):

Find a quiet place where you can be uninterrupted for a few minutes. Have your child sit or lie down and close her eyes or keep them open and stare at a spot on the floor. Read the following slowly and softly to your child:

Start breathing in and out, inhaling and exhaling slowly, paying attention to your breath, going in and out … in and out. (After a few moments of breathing in and out very deeply) … the next time you breathe in, follow your breath all the way down deep inside to the center of your body. Let your breath come in and warm you. As you let it out, let your body relax even more. You are comfortable here in this place. It's all yours. You are safe here. You can rest here free from worry or pressure. It is warm, it is free, it is still.

Still breathing, you're invited to explore and find a place deep inside … a place that is yours and yours alone. (Pause a few seconds.) Have you found it? Where is it? What is it like? Is there anything around you? How do you make it your own? You rest quietly here for a while, breathing slowly, deeply, and peacefully. This place is here and will always be here just for you. It is inside you and you can come here whenever you like and stay here as long as you like. Here you can hear the deepest yearnings of your heart. Here you can hear truth. As you rest here, safe and secure, is your heart telling you anything? Does it have any messages? There is no right or wrong answer, only your experience. Continue to breathe slowly, bringing your breath down to meet you where you are, and as you let it go, let it take anything you don't need there.

Continue to listen for the voice of your heart. (Pause.) When you're ready, slowly follow your breath all the way up … and exhale … knowing that you can return to this place, your very own place anytime you choose. As you continue to exhale, very slowly, gently open your eyes.

C. "THE JOURNEY WITHIN" (CHILDREN TEN AND UP):

Just as in the previous exercise, begin by getting into a comfortable position, sitting in a quiet place where you are uninterrupted for a few minutes. Begin by breathing slowly, paying attention to your breath, going in and out … in and out.

Now picture a beautiful place that's all your own. It may be a place you're been to before, or it may be a totally new place. Wherever it is, it's a place where you feel safe and secure. You love it here. As you look around, what do you see? Are there plants and trees? Are there mountains or is there water? What is the weather like? What colors do you see? What sounds do you hear? What do you smell? Find places to run and play, here in your very own place.

Looking up, you see a large friendly animal standing on a rock. You are delighted to see this animal. You know this animal is here to help guide you and be your companion. The animal welcomes you to this place, and together you begin to walk on a path. You decide to see where it goes.

As you walk along the path, you notice everything around you. What do you see? Does the scenery change? How are you feeling as you walk along? After a while, you come to an intersection on the path. There are several ways you could go. You have a choice. Which path should you take? You are not worried because each way leads to a place that is full of good things just for you. There is no wrong decision. You ask your animal guide, which way you should take. You understand that this guide will go with you whichever way you take, that you will not be alone. You trust that this guide wants the best for you. What does your guide tell you? Deep inside, you know your guide is right.

You thank your guide. Together you begin down the path with confidence that good things are ahead for you.

Now it is time to say good-bye to your guide for the time being. Your guide will always be there for you whenever you need him/her. You can call on him/her at any time. But now it is time to come back here into this room. You know that this same confidence and good feeling will stay with you throughout your day… and when you are ready, slowly open your eyes.

If you like, you can keep a journal to write down your experiences. It's amazing when we give ourselves the time and space to journey within, what clues and direction we can receive – and it's there for us all the time!

Peyton's Point of View
Ommm. Ommmmm. (Laugh) I only like meditation because you get to say, Ommmmm! It helps you relax and just be in your body and you can listen to God and see if you can help Him. It can help you if you're nervous before a test or something.

Questions for Reflection:
1. If you participated in any of these exercises, which one did you like the best and why?
2. What was your experience like?
3. Did you learn anything about yourself as a result of doing this?
4. Have you found a place inside yourself which is safe, where you feel comfortable going when you need to? If not, do you know why?
5. Which of your senses was most powerful? Sight, sound, smell, touch, taste?
6. What changes would you make to any of these exercises? Go ahead and make them!
7. Do you want to share what your guide is like?

Sacred Spaces

A sanctuary is a place that is safe and special to you. It may be a special place in your house, up in a tree house, or out in nature somewhere. My rabbi friend says we create sacred spaces. In Judaism the first sanctuaries or sacred spaces were out in the desert, when the children of Israel were wandering after leaving

Egypt. She says that it wasn't the space itself which was sacred; it was what was done in the space which made it sacred.

A sanctuary is also what worship spaces are called in a Church, Synagogue or Mosque. They are places where people come to pray, talk, sing and listen to God. People generally talk softly to honor God and in consideration of others who may be trying to pray. Sometimes, people take off their shoes in their place of worship, to pay respect and to show that the space is different from other places.

I took Peyton with a group from my congregation to experience a worship service at a Sufi Mosque one time. We looked at all of the shoes when we went into the mosque.

Peyton also noticed that the women and girls were asked to wear scarves over their heads. In some religions, both men and women wear some sort of head covering as a sign of respect for God.

Try This: Creating A Sacred Space
How about creating your own sacred space? I have a little altar in my office that I use as a place to center my thoughts. It has candles and sacred keepsakes from different periods of my life. When I sit in front of it, I am able to find peace and a sense of calm. It is my own sacred space, my sanctuary in my home, and it helps me think of God.

By encouraging our children to create their own sanctuaries externally, it can help them to create a sense of sacred space *within* themselves; a place which is always accessible to them whenever they need to find a place of peace.

Peyton's Point of View
It's important to have a place where you can go and just be yourself and get your feelings out. If you've had a bad day and you're able to go to that special place, you can think about what

happened and be able to say, "I did the right thing today."

Questions for Reflection:
1. What are some places that feel special or "sacred" to you?
2. Where do you feel the safest?
3. How can I help you create a space that is a sanctuary here at home?
4. What elements need to be part of that space?
5. When you go to your house of worship, what things do you do that show it is a sacred space?

Dreams of the Future

From very early in life, the question, "What do you want to be when you grow up?" is asked of most children by inquisitive parents. Certainly no one is holding a four-year-old to the answer, but ideas and dreams are often formed early in life and can be seen through play or interests. Peyton's answer to the question has ranged from a combination of her father's and my professions to those of people she admires.

Many children don't know what they want to be, but giving them the room and space to dream out loud without an "Oh, no you're not!" from a parent is important.

My parents always told me I could be whatever I wanted to be and do whatever I wanted to do. That is, until I wanted to teach in the Philippines for a while after college. That's when they said, "Oh, no you're not!" That was because the Philippines were under Marshall Law at the time. The freedom to dream and explore my different passions allowed me to find out who I was becoming and follow my dreams as they developed.

Questions to help learn about your child's dreams might be asked in creative ways, through a diary, an art project, a volunteer opportunity, or a conversation after a school presentation of parents' professions. You can follow up with questions such as, "What is it about that profession that makes you want to be one?" A parent can also help their children with insights they have about them. Perhaps the child says they want to be a doctor or a nurse. You might respond this way: "You are very kind and compassionate around people. That suits you." Or if they say they want to be a veterinary technician, you might say, "I know you love animals very much, and you care for them well." Or if they want to be a trash collector, "You really care about keeping the earth clean." Or if they want to be a teacher, "You really are good with children and are patient." What's important is not to tell them what *you* want for them, even if you're screaming it out inside. By letting them find their own way, you keep the doors of conversation open. Continue to teach them to know themselves so they can explore and do something they love in the future.

Today most people will retrain at least once in their lives to prepare for another type of profession. It is rare to find people who stay with the same company or even industry their entire career, like many in our parents' and grandparents' generations. Job loss, shifting trends in the market place, technological advances, changing personal interests, and the mobility of people in our society are all reasons people shift careers. The more parents can be open to their child's exploration of who they are and how they can contribute to the working world, the better. Not everyone knows without question what they want to do for the rest of their lives by the time they begin working. Bless those who *do* know from an early age and remain in that field for their entire professional lives. They can build an extensive volume of experience and a loyal clientele that is nearly impossible to gain without time. For some, their lives may involve taking part in family businesses which have rich traditions in the community. The important point is to make sure your child knows they have a choice in what they want to be in the future.

I know a man who was encouraged from childhood to be an oral surgeon. As a good son, he pursued that profession and became quite successful, providing well for his family. But, even though he did well financially and helped many people over the years, deep down inside he didn't like what he was doing. Finally, when he was in his fifties he decided to see a career counselor and do some testing to discover what his natural gifts were. The tests showed he was suited for web design and he had been overcompensating for years in a profession which was not suited for him. He now runs a successful web design firm and is deeply fulfilled.

I have trained for three careers in my life: banking, ministry, and journalism. Each move has brought out different strengths and has contributed not only to my professional life, but to my personal life as well. If I had stayed in banking, which I pursued because that's what my father did, I would have been miserable. I am so grateful for parents who encouraged me to pursue my dreams!

Peyton's Point of View
It's great to have choices, because if you have only one choice, you may not like it in the future. Say you want to be an elephant poop picker-upper. When you get older, you may think an elephant poop picker-upper is not so great.

(Note: for all of the elephant poop picker-uppers of the world, please know this is only a metaphor!)

Questions for Reflection (for parents):
1. What were the messages you received as a child about your future working life?
2. What, if any, expectations were there? (For me, it was expected that after college, I was not going to live at home so needed to have launched my career by that time.)
3. What messages were given about college or graduate school?

4. Was it the same for the boys in the house as the girls?
5. What are your hopes for your child in terms of educational level?
6. What are your hopes for your child in terms of a career path?
7. What do you see as your child's natural gifts?
8. Are there ways you can encourage the further development of those gifts now?

Questions for Reflection (for children):
1. How important is school to you?
2. What opportunities do you think getting an education gives someone?
3. Who are the people out in the community you most admire?
4. What do they do for a living?
5. Could you see yourself doing that some day?
6. Do you feel the freedom to be what you want to be? Why or why not?
7. Do you know what it will it take to do what you want to do?
8. What kind of education do you need or will be helpful for that?

Conclusion

As parents, we have one of the most challenging yet rewarding jobs in the world: raising our children. It's even more difficult today than for our parents, because of the outside influences and potential dangers that lurk beyond what we can see. But I say, *bring it on*! Nothing can be more exciting and life-giving than embracing each day and growing along the way together, blasting through fear and grabbing on to the extravagant gifts of grace and love.

When I was beginning the process of international adoption, another single mother who had two adopted girls told me, "Your daughter is out there, somewhere, waiting for you to come and get her." Those words were so soothing to me. They reminded me that whether through birth or adoption, there is no accident involved

in our relationships with our children. Each of us has the child/
children we are meant to have in this lifetime. Our children will
bring us the lessons we need to learn, and we will give them the
love and lessons we have to give that are unique to those relationships. That is a miracle to me.

Certainly there is pain at times. No parent is perfect. No child
is perfect. Thank God for that. Somehow as we walk along this
journey of life, may we see our humanity a bit more clearly. May
we accept that the life we have been given together is one worth
living more fully and loving more deeply.

Thank you for letting us explore some of our ideas with you.
"Take what you like and leave the rest!" We'd love to hear your
feedback as well as your stories. Please visit us at our website,
www.shannonawhite.com.

We salute you!
Shannon and Peyton White

Bibliography
Referenced in Book

Bradshaw, John. *Healing the Shame That Binds You* (Health Communications, Deerfield Beach, Florida, 1988)

By Kids for Kids, Famous Inventors
(http://www.bkfk.com/inventor/inventors.asp)

Dinkmeyer, Don, Sr., McKay, Gary, Dinkmeyer, Don, Jr., *The Parent's Handbook: Systematic Training for Effective Parenting* (STEP Publishers, www.STEPPublishers.com, 1997)

Ganley, Theodore with Sherman, Carl. *Exercise and Children's Health: A Little Counseling Can Pay Lasting Dividends Practical tips for age-appropriate activity and lifetime fitness.* (The Physician and Sportsmedicine: Volume 28: No.2, February 2000 http://www.physsportsmed.com/index.php?art=psm_02_2000?article=699)

Guerrero, Diana, *What Animals Can Teach Us about Spirituality: Inspiring Lessons from Wild and Tame Creatures* (SkyLight Paths Publishing 2006, Woodstock, Vermont www.skylightpaths.com)

Hoffman, Bob, *The Negative Love Syndrome and the Quadrinity Model: A Path to Personal Freedom and Love* (The Hoffman Institute USA, San Rafael, CA, 1984)

Laughter Yoga (http://www.laughteryoga.org/)

Learning Disabilities in Children: Learning Disability Symptoms, Types, and Testing (Helpguide.org, http://www.helpguide.org/mental/learning_disabilities.htm)

Marijuana: Facts for Teens, National Institute of Drug Abuse: The Science of Drug Abuse, (NIH Publication No. 04-4037, Revised March 2008 (http://www.drugabuse.gov/marijBroch/teenpg3-4. html#many)

National Crime Prevention Council, (http://www.ncpc.org/ newsroom/current-campaigns/cyberbullying)

Orman, Suze. *What Money Has Taught Me About Personal Power* (O Magazine, September 2009)

Rumi, selected and translated by Helminski, Camille and Kabir, *Jewels of Remembrance* (Reprinted by arrangement with Shambhala Publications Inc. 2006, Boston, MA. www.shambhala.com)

Shoplifting Statistics, (National Shoplifting Prevention Coalition, http://www.shopliftingprevention.org/WhatNASPOffers/NRC/ PublicEducStats.htm)

Torgan, Carol. *Childhood Obesity on the Rise* (The NIH Word on Health, June 2002 http://www.nih.gov/news/WordonHealth/ jun2002/childhoodobesity.htm)

Violent Video Games: Psychologists Help Protect Children from Harmful Effects (American Psychological Association 2004 http:// www.apa.org/research/action/games.aspx)

What is cyberbullying, exactly? (Stopcyberbullying.org, the cyber-bullying prevention site operated by WiredSafety.org. http://www. stopcyberbullying.org/what_is_cyberbullying_exactly.html)

World Laughter Day (http://www.worldlaughterday.org/)

RESEARCH REFERENCES

Clurman, Ruth-Ann, *Parenting the Other Chick's Eggs* (National Press Publications, Shawnee Mission, Kansas, 1997)

Cohn, Janice *The Christmas Menorahs: How a Town Fought Hate* (Albert Whitman and Company, 1995, Morton Grove, Illinois).

Comstock, Kani and Marisa Thame, *Journey Into Love: Ten Steps to Wholeness* (Willow Press, Ashland, Oregon, 2000)

Faber, Adele and Elaine Mazlish, *How to Talk So Kids Will Listen and Listen So Kids Will Talk* (Quill, New York, 2002)

Joseph, Joanne M., *The Resilient Child: Preparing Today's Youth for Tomorrow's World* (Insight Books, Plenum Press, New York, 1994)

Kiyosaki, Robert, Lechter, Sharon L. *Rich Dad, Poor Dad* (Warner Books in association with Cashflow Technologies Inc., New York, 2008)

Kushner, Harold S., *How Good Do We Have to Be?* (Little, Brown and Company, New York, 1996)

Masoff, Joy, *Oh, Yuck: The Encyclopedia of Everything Nasty* (Workman Publishing, New York, 2000)

Rubadeau, Joan, *The Little Book of Good: Spiritual Values for Parents and Children* (PAGL Press, 1986)

Wolf, Anthony E., Ph.D., *Get Out of My Life But First Could You Take Me and Cheryl To The Mall?* (Farrar Straus Giroux, New York, 1991)

Zukov, Gary and Linda Francis, *The Heart of the Soul: Emotional Awareness* (Simon and Schuster Source, New York, 2001)

RECOMMENDATIONS

Camps for Kids in Need
Camp Erin, for children who have lost a parent through death.
http://www.moyerfoundation.org/events/erin.aspx

Operation Purple, camps and retreats for children and families of the military.
http://www.militaryfamily.org/our-programs/operation-purple/

Hole in the Wall Gang Camp (Paul Newman's camp), for children dealing with cancer and other life-threatening illnesses, including Double H Ranch and others.
www.holeinthewallgangcamp.org

Programs for Personal Growth
The Hoffman Institute, San Rafael, CA, with East Coast satellites
An eight-day intensive retreat which aims to resolve seemingly immovable blocks to emotional freedom, family issues, well-being and more.
www.hoffmaninstitute.org

The Caron Foundation, Wernersville, PA
A treatment program for alcohol, drug abuse, co-dependency and other addictions.
www.caron.org

Peak Potentials, T. Harv Eker, international events
 Seminars, courses and camps for personal success.
www.peakpotentials.com

Keys to the Vault, Keith Cunningham, international events
Personal and business growth courses achieving financial success:
Business Mastery, 4 Day MBA program, How to Buy a Business.
www.keystothevault.com

Vemma Nutritional Products
Vemma stands for Vitamins, Essential Minerals, Mangosteen and
Aloe. It is a liquid daily supplement which provides a complete
multi-vitamin for children through adults. It's antioxidant rich and
tastes delicious. For a full listing of Vemma products, go to www.
shannonwhite.vemma.com/
(In an effort toward full disclosure, Shannon and Peyton own this
site and will benefit from any sales.)

Thank you...from Shannon

Just as it takes a village to raise a child, it also takes a village to write a book. Without the help of many people, you would not be reading these words.

First, thank you to my mother and Peyton's grandmother, Ellen, who is a shining example of a woman who overcame many obstacles to live fully and is dedicated to her girls. She teaches me to use my gifts and talents in this world with grace.

To my father Bob, who encouraged me to strive for excellence in all things. Without you, Dad, I would not be the woman I am today.

To my sisters who are all strong, independent women doing great things in the world. I especially thank Heather, who was the first to look at this unedited work and didn't laugh! Liz Hunt was the second, thank you for your generosity.

I could never have completed this book without Donna Cravotta, my virtual assistant. Donna, your encouragement, organization, creativity, and great sense of humor are terrific. Kim Pearson, my editor, had fabulous suggestions for my text and made the words pop. Pete Friedrich of Charette designed the interior and stunning cover. Thank you for many hours of dedication on this project. Thanks also to Nicolle Kaufmann for taking great pictures which capture the spirit of youth, to Phil Callaci of Peanut Portraits for our headshots, and to Wendy VanHatten, my proofreader. Tom Mahoney was a great resource for several sections of this book. Tom, your honest and frank way helps people accept their humanity.

Thank you to all of the mothers, fathers, children, friends, and congregants who allowed us to use their stories and pictures in this work. Your stories keep this work honest and real.

Thank you to my mentors: Cheshta Buckley and Joel Baehr, for seeing me through the Hoffman Process and into a more integrated life; Keith Cunningham for supporting this work and reigniting my entrepreneurial spirit along with our Business Mastery class...especially Elaine who kept me on my game daily during the writing process; and to Beth Wright and Reese, who kept my energy flowing in a positive direction.

Thank you all.

About the Authors

Shannon A. White

Shannon is an author, pastor, speaker and coach to those who want to live with greater integrity, authenticity, and compassion. Her training and many professional roles have helped shape who she is.

She received her educational degrees from Auburn University (BA, Business Admin) and Princeton Theological Seminary (MDiv). In 1991, she was ordained in the Presbyterian Church (USA) and has served as minister and assistant minister of several churches in New York and Connecticut spanning 13 years. She co-hosted "Spirit-Talk," a radio show with a rabbi colleague, interviewing people of different spiritual backgrounds. She then brought her interest to television, first behind-the-scenes at CBS News in the Religion Unit. She was production assistant and then associate producer, creating four interfaith documentaries a year. She then pursued on-camera work at News 12 Westchester, a 24-hour cable news station in suburban New York. She has received multiple awards for her feature reporting on issues such as: alcoholism/addiction and spirituality at Sing Sing Correctional Facility.

Shannon's most important role, however, is as a mother to her 10-year-old daughter. She says, "Nothing is more challenging or re-warding than to support the healthy growth of a child in this world. Shannon embraces this daunting task with fear and excitement.

Peyton White

Peyton White is a 5th Grade elementary student who loves basket-ball, snowboarding, playing with friends, and her Nintendo DS. She also enjoys travelling with her mom to interesting areas of the world. She loves her brothers and sisters...and her adorable dog, Max.

Shannon, Peyton and Max live in Westchester County, a suburb of New York.

"Shannon addresses all the difficult and challenging issues of family life in today's world with candor, honesty, thoughtfulness, and humor. Her personal reflections and revelations resonate in the hearts and souls of everyone who has ever been a parent or a child, a husband or a wife, a brother or a sister."
—Rabbi Vicki L. Axe, DM, RJE

"I think most people do not put much thought into parenting; they tend to imitate their parents. Many of the topics you cover used to be the realm of grandmothers. Now grandmothers are too far away to be a daily influence in many situations or just not in touch with current ways of thinking. You have done a terrific job of picking subjects and examples and stepping in for grandma.
This is a perfect book for young parents; I will give it as a baby shower gift going forward.
—Patty Oliveira, mother

Notes